Social Issues
in Literature

War in Stephen Crane's
The Red Badge of Courage

Other Books in the Social Issues in Literature Series:

Social Issues
in Literature

War in Stephen Crane's
The Red Badge of Courage

David Haugen and Susan Musser, Book Editors

GREENHAVEN PRESS
A part of Gale, Cengage Learning

GALE
CENGAGE Learning

Detroit • New York • San Francisco • New Haven, Conn • Waterville, Maine • London

Christine Nasso, *Publisher*
Elizabeth Des Chenes, *Managing Editor*

© 2010 Greenhaven Press, a part of Gale, Cengage Learning

Gale and Greenhaven Press are registered trademarks used herein under license.

For more information, contact:
Greenhaven Press
27500 Drake Rd.
Farmington Hills, MI 48331-3535
Or you can visit our Internet site at gale.cengage.com

For product information and technology assistance, contact us at

Gale Customer Support, 1-800-877-4253
For permission to use material from this text or product, submit all requests online at
www.cengage.com/permissions

Further permissions questions can be emailed to permissionrequest@cengage.com

Articles in Greenhaven Press anthologies are often edited for length to meet page requirements. In addition, original titles of these works are changed to clearly present the main thesis and to explicitly indicate the author's opinion. Every effort is made to ensure that Greenhaven Press accurately reflects the original intent of the authors. Every effort has been made to trace the owners of copyrighted material.

Cover image from Hulton Archive/Getty Images.

LIBRARY OF CONGRESS CATALOGING-IN-PUBLICATION DATA

War in Stephen Crane's The red badge of courage / David Haugen and Susan Musser, book editors.
    p. cm. -- (Social issues in literature)
    Includes bibliographical references and index.
    ISBN 978-0-7377-4850-5 -- ISBN 978-0-7377-4851-2 (pbk.)
    1. Crane, Stephen, 1871-1900. Red badge of courage. 2. War in literature. 3. United States--History--Civil War, 1861-1865--Literature and the war. I. Haugen, David M., 1969- II. Musser, Susan.
    PS1449.C85R399 2010
    813'.4--dc22
                                  2009045224

Printed in the United States of America
1 2 3 4 5 6 7 14 13 12 11 10

Contents

Chapter 1: Background on Stephen Crane

James B. Colvert

As a writer, Stephen Crane gravitated toward gritty, realistic topics that exposed the harsh sides of life; however, he did not agree with all the tenets of literary realism, and he eventually tried to distance himself from the novel that had both secured his fame and his rank as a master realist writer.

Ken Chowder

Although Crane had not participated in the war that he wrote about in *The Red Badge of Courage*, he did become a combat journalist covering subsequent international conflicts. In those endeavors, he earned a reputation for his adventuresome spirit and for his bravery in the midst of action.

Chapter 2: *The Red Badge of Courage* and War

Harold Hungerford

Clues within *The Red Badge of Courage* and another story concerning Crane's main character, Henry Fleming, indicate that Fleming earned his "red badge" at the Battle of Chancellorsville, a bloody confrontation in Virginia during the spring of 1863.

Perry Lentz

Stephen Crane debunked the myth that soldiers in the midst of battle are concerned with the righteousness of their cause and adherence to the discipline instilled by their training. Henry Fleming thinks of neither loyalty nor commands when in battle; his mind is on self-preservation and the bruise to his ego that comes from an act of cowardice.

Chapter 3: Contemporary Perspectives on War

Introduction

Stephen Crane was born in 1871, six years after the South's surrender that ended the bloodiest war in U.S. history. It may seem ironic, then, that Crane would write what many regard as the definitive novel about the American Civil War. He was twenty-one or twenty-two years old when he began drafting *The Red Badge of Courage*, his most famous book. Upon its publication in 1895, many critics praised its wartime realism. Harold Frederic, the London editor of the *New York Times*, wrote in his January 1896 review that "*The Red Badge* impels the feeling that the actual truth about a battle has never been guessed before." Frederic even notes that other contemporary reviewers took it for granted that "the writer of the *Red Badge* must have seen real warfare." Of course, Stephen Crane had not. Although he would later become a war journalist covering actions in Cuba and Greece, the young author of *The Red Badge of Courage* had not experienced a military engagement during the composition of his Civil War masterpiece.

Despite not being an eyewitness to the conflict that shaped his novel, Crane was—as scholar Harold R. Hungerford claims—likely privy to the reminiscences of veterans who had fought in the Union ranks. "Many middle-aged men in Port Jervis [New York, where Crane lived as a youth,] had served in the 124th New York," Hungerford writes. "It is hard to believe that men in an isolated small town could have resisted telling a hero-worshipping small boy about a great adventure in their lives." In addition, as Hungerford and others have pointed out, Crane had read *Battles and Leaders of the Civil War*, a series of recollections of both Northern and Southern military men published in the late 1880s, in preparation for his novel. All of these soldiers' tales—both oral and written—probably gave Crane some insight into the trials of a soldier's life as well as the hoped-for glories of combat.

Although factual resources undoubtedly aided in the creation of *The Red Badge of Courage*, Crane did not simply engage in reportage to bring to life the nineteenth-century battlefield. As British critic George Wyndham, one of the champions of Crane's novel, stated in his review of the book, the singular experiences of battle—tragic and triumphant—are "the things which even dull men remember with the undying imagination of poets, but which, for lack of the writer's art, they cannot communicate." In Wyndham's opinion, Crane succeeded in conveying "the new things [a soldier] has heard and seen and felt." As Wyndham maintains,

> You may shut the book, but you still see the battle-flags "jerked about madly in the smoke," or sinking with "dying gestures of despair," the men "dropping here and there like bundles"; the captain shot dead with "an astonished and sorrowful look as if he thought some friend had done him an ill-turn"; and the litter of corpses, "twisted in fantastic contortions," as if "they had fallen from some great height, dumped out upon the ground from the sky." The book is full of sensuous impressions that leap out from the picture: of gestures, attitudes, grimaces, that flash into portentous definition, like faces from the climbing clouds of nightmare. It leaves the imagination bounded with a "dense wall of smoke, furiously slit and slashed by the knife-like fire from the rifles." It leaves, in short, such indelible traces as are left by the actual experience of war.

These "sensuous impressions" are what make some critics dub *The Red Badge of Courage* an impressionist, rather than a realist, novel. Readers glimpse the battlefield through the limited impressions of Crane's protagonist, Union private Henry Fleming, a youth who is untested and unfamiliar with the sights and sounds of war when he steps into his first fight. As modern critic James Nagel explains, "Henry's view of the battle is severely limited. He knows nothing of the strategy of the battle; he frequently cannot interpret the events around him because his information is obscured by darkness, smoke, or the noise of cannons." Most reviewers believe this restricted perception makes the experience of warfare more intense, emphasizing the impact of terror upon the common soldier—especially those, like Henry Fleming, who were callow volunteers.

Fleming's sensory confusion on the battlefield is often more than disorientation. When he faces the enemy for the first time, he cannot recall whether he has loaded his rifle. He fights that first fight in a state of rage, wishing to rush forward to strangle the oncoming Confederates because his rifle could not react fast enough to match his heated emotions. As the first wave of attackers is beaten off, Fleming revels in his heroism. Yet as a second enemy line advances, Fleming—taken aback because the fight had not ended and struck impotent because his ferocity had not, in "a world-sweeping gesture," kept the enemy at bay—gives into fear and flees from the undaunted foe. It is this moment of weakness that made Crane's novel a subject of controversy in its day.

In 1896, after *The Red Badge of Courage* was receiving praise from overseas reviewers and going into a second printing in America, General Alexander C. McClurg, a military man who marched with Union general William T. Sherman as he drove a deep wedge into the Southern lines late in the Civil War, repudiated the truthfulness of Crane's supposed realism. In a letter to the *Dial* magazine, he referred to the book as "the vain imaginings of a young man born long since that war." Calling the character of Fleming "an ignorant and stupid country lad ... without a spark of patriotic feeling," McClurg denounces him and his comrades as cowards who do not possess the sense of duty and love of country owned by "the quiet, manly, self-respecting, and patriotic men ... who in reality fought our battles." English critics, however, were quick to back Crane's work, insisting that the story aptly illustrated the impressions and reactions of volunteers who were working on farms or in businesses one day and plunked down in battle lines seemingly overnight.

Today, more than a century after the publication of *The Red Badge of Courage*, scholars tend to view Crane's war novel as an antiwar novel. The heroism that Henry Fleming eventually claims for himself after returning from his flight and bravely fighting in a subsequent engagement is most often assumed to be ironic, for his motivations still have nothing to do with patriotism or even a close regard for his comrades. While some view this exhibition of courage as exemplifying Fleming's maturation over two days of combat, most reviewers insist that the manhood Fleming aspires to (perhaps even achieves) is based on chivalric notions still popular in adventure novels of Crane's day. And it is these romanticized plotlines that Crane ostensibly undercuts by matching Fleming's youthful fancies with the morbid realities of death and squalor. In essence, Crane's view of war is not idealized even if his character's perspective is. It is this tension, however, that still attracts readers to this book. The battlefield continues to elicit feelings of excitement, valor, and idealism from observers and participants in spite of the fact that war entails cowardice, moral ambiguity, and the finality of death.

Chronology

1871

Stephen Townley Crane is born in Newark, New Jersey, to the Reverend Jonathan Townley Crane and Mary Helen Peck.

1878

After moving around New Jersey because of his father's changing pastorate appointments, Crane's family settles in Port Jervis, New York. Crane enters school for the first time.

1880

Crane's father dies.

1883

Crane's mother moves the family to Asbury Park, New Jersey.

1888

Crane attends a military boarding school in Claverack, New York. During his summer holidays, he writes articles for his brother Townley who runs a news outlet for the *New York Tribune*.

1891

Crane enrolls in Syracuse University but eventually leaves school to pursue a writing career. He frequents the Bowery of New York City to study the seedier sides of life. He makes his living, though, by writing sketches of the summer guests who flock to the beaches and hotels along the Asbury shore. These he publishes regularly in the *Tribune*. His mother dies late in the year.

1892

After offending his publisher, Crane loses his stint as a sketch writer. He tries to elicit interest in a short novel, *Maggie: A Girl of the Streets*, that arose from his Bowery studies. Finding no interest—due to the story's vivid and brutal portrayal of street life, Crane self-publishes the novel under a pseudonym the following year. The book sells poorly.

1893

Crane reads *Battles and Leaders of the Civil War* and other Civil War stories as research for a new novel that he begins in the spring.

1894

With encouragement from critics, Crane sends his completed manuscript for *The Red Badge of Courage* to S.S. McClure, a prominent publisher. While waiting for a response, Crane drafts his next novel, *George's Mother*, another story of Bowery life. He writes other stories and poems throughout the year. In October, Crane retrieves his *Red Badge* manuscript from McClure—who is still undecided—and sells the work to a syndicator who has the novel serialized in various newspapers. Its success in newsprint leads to a book contract in December.

1895

The Red Badge of Courage is published by D. Appleton and Company. Based on the favorable reception of the novel, Appleton reprints *Maggie*. A London publishing house publishes *George's Mother*. Crane's first collection of poems, *The Black Riders, and Other Lines*, also reaches print.

1896

Now a literary celebrity, Crane gets caught up in the trial of a chorus girl accused of prostitution. Crane agrees to give testimony in her defense. She is exonerated, but Crane's reputation is soiled by reporters who link the writer to a morally questionable lifestyle. *The Little Regiment and Other Episodes of the American Civil War*, a collection of short stories containing a Henry Fleming narrative titled "The Veteran," is published by Appleton.

1897

Having taken a job as a war correspondent covering the war in Cuba, Crane is shipwrecked at sea when the steamship *Commodore* hits a sandbar and sinks on the voyage out from Florida. The experience lays the groundwork for his famed short story, "The Open Boat." The ordeal also exacerbates his tuberculosis, a disease he has been carrying since his days in New York City. When other efforts to reach Cuba fail, Crane is sent to Greece to cover the Greco-Turkish War. He travels to Greece with Cora Taylor, a hotel manager, whom he marries during their stay.

1898

After the Greco-Turkish War appointment, Crane and his wife spend time in England. There, he writes "The Blue Hotel," another well-received short story published serially in *Collier's Weekly*. Crane is feted by many writers in England; privately, though, his debts and poor financial dealings have left him in near poverty. He returns alone to the States in February to work as a war correspondent in the Spanish-American War. He sees action in Cuba, covering such engagements as Teddy Roosevelt's Rough Riders' and other American troops' storming of San Juan Hill.

1899

Having returned to his wife in England, Crane continues to spend more than he earns. He takes on all manner of writing assignments to make money. He begins work on *The O'Ruddy*, an Irish romance novel that he never completes. *War Is Kind*, his second poetry collection, is published in the United States. In December, Crane suffers a hemorrhage in the lungs due to his worsening tuberculosis.

1900

Trying to fulfill writing commitments to stave off debtors, Crane ignores his health. In May he and his wife travel to a spa in Badenweiler, Germany, for treatment. He dies there on June 5 and is later buried in New Jersey.

Social Issues
in Literature

CHAPTER 1

Background on
Stephen Crane

Stephen Crane and His Realistic War Fable

James B. Colvert

James B. Colvert is a now-retired professor of literature at the University of Georgia. He has written a biography of Stephen Crane as well as the introductions to collections of Crane's work and scholarly essays on The Red Badge of Courage. *Colvert has also served on the editorial board of the Stephen Crane Society.*

Stephen Crane was a gifted writer who at a young age worked for New Jersey and New York newspapers covering the manners and morals of both the wealthy seaside vacationers and the poor of New York City. His preference for describing the gritty realism of slum life led to the drafting of Maggie: A Girl of the Streets, *a novel that publishers rejected for its lurid realism. In the following viewpoint, Colvert contends that this same unromantic bent later produced Crane's well-received novel* The Red Badge of Courage, *a work that critics found largely to be a realistic portrayal of combat during the American Civil War. Although Crane's reputation was made by that novel, Colvert states that Crane felt limited by the "badge" he had earned as a Realist. Crane had never taken part in the war, and he disliked being termed an authority on the subject. He confessed that he would rather be recognized as a writer who dealt with the whole scope of life. According to Colvert, many critics have noted the manner in which experience and environment shape the individual and the restricted perception of the characters in relating these elements to the reader. For these reasons, some have linked Crane to literary impressionism while not denying his objective, realist underpinnings.*

James B. Colvert, "Stephen Crane," in *Dictionary of Literary Biography, vol. 12, American Realists and Naturalists*, edited by Donald Pizer and Earl N. Harbert, Detroit: Gale Research, 1982. Copyright © 1982 by Gale Research. Copyright © 2007 Gale, Cengage Learning. Reproduced by permission of Gale, a part of Cengage Learning.

A precursor of the imagists in poetry and of the novelists writing the new fiction of the 1920s, Stephen Crane was one of the most gifted and influential writers of the late nineteenth century, noted for his brilliant and innovative style, his vivid, ironic sense of life, and his penetrating psychological realism. Unusually precocious, he wrote his first novel, *Maggie: A Girl of the Streets* (1893), when he was only twenty-one and had his masterpiece, *The Red Badge of Courage* (1895), published before he was twenty-four. When he died in 1900 at the age of twenty-eight, from tuberculosis and the effects of his exhausting life as adventurer and war correspondent, he had written, in addition to his voluminous war reportage and numerous incidental pieces, six novels, well over a hundred stories and sketches, and two books of poems—enough all together to fill ten large volumes in the University Press of Virginia edition of his collected works. Neglected for two decades after his death, he was rediscovered in the 1920s by poets and novelists (such as Amy Lowell, Willa Cather, Sherwood Anderson, and Joseph Hergesheimer) who recognized in his experiments with new subjects, themes, and forms something of the spirit of their own literary aims.

Although these aims were derived originally from such nineteenth-century realists as Hamlin Garland, William Dean Howells, Rudyard Kipling, [Leo] Tolstoy, and others of perhaps more indeterminant influence, he radically altered their principles and methods to serve his own unique vision and purposes. He eschewed the conventional plot, shifting the focus from the drama of external event or situation to the drama of thought and feeling in the mental life of his subjects. He substituted for the conventional expository, descriptive style a highly metaphorical, imagistic representation of psychological effects. And he denied, in his most telling work, assumptions about norms of reality, often depicting unfolding experience as gradual revelation of its ultimate mystery. A relativist, ironist, and impressionist, he anticipated the modernism of

[Ernest] Hemingway, [F. Scott] Fitzgerald, [Sherwood] Anderson, and [William] Faulkner by thirty years. Like Hemingway, he was preoccupied with violence, finding in the reaction of his hero under the stress of ultimate crisis the mystery and poignancy of the hero's character and fate. Like Anderson, Fitzgerald, and Faulkner, he dramatized the powers of illusion to shape events and destinies. He does, indeed, seem closer to these writers in manner and spirit than to the writers of his own day.

A Minister's Son

The experience which contributed most importantly to the shaping of Crane's modernist ideas and attitude was probably his early life as a minister's son. He was born 1 November 1871, in Newark, New Jersey, the last of fourteen children of the Reverend Dr. Jonathan Townley Crane, a well-known Methodist clergyman, and Mary Helen Peck Crane. Mrs. Crane, a descendant of a long line of Methodist preachers "of the old ambling-nag, saddle-bag, exhorting kind" (as Crane once described them), was active in church and reform work, serving at one time as an officer in the New Jersey Women's Christian Temperance Union. Her uncle, the Reverend Jesse Peck, a Methodist bishop and one of the founders of Syracuse University, was the author of a minatory religious treatise "redolent with the fumes of sulphur and brimstone," *What Must I Do to Be Saved?* (1858), a copy of which Stephen Crane inherited from his father in 1881. The bishop's view of God as a God of wrath was apparently shared, to some extent at least, by Crane's mother; but his father, who resigned from the Presbyterian church as a young man in protest against the harshness of its doctrine of infant damnation, was apparently of a gentler persuasion, stressing in his milder books on Christian conduct a view of God as a God of mercy and compassion. The religious poems in Stephen Crane's first book of poems, *The Black Riders* (1895), written about the same time he was writing *The Red Badge of Courage*, reflect the anguish of a spiritual crisis in which he attempted to exorcise the Pecks' God of wrath and, beyond that, to test his faith in general against the moral realities he observed as a young newspaper reporter in Asbury Park, New Jersey, and New York City in the early 1890s. The religious issue haunted Crane's imagination to the end. As Amy Lowell observed, "He disbelieved it and hated it, but he could not free himself from it." The effect of his preoccupation with questions of faith is not only evident in his poetry but appears, more obliquely, in his fiction as well, notably in its striking evocation of man's poignant alienation in a God-abandoned world of menace and violence.

Two years after his father died in 1880, Mrs. Crane moved to Asbury Park, New Jersey, a popular resort town on the coast where one of his older brothers, Townley, operated a news agency for the *New York Tribune*. Left much to his own devices, since Mrs. Crane was often busy with church and reform projects, Stephen roamed the beaches, indulged his passion for baseball (one of the pastimes his father cautioned against in his book *Popular Amusements*, 1869), and under the influence of his mentor Townley and another older brother, Will, who advised him once to ignore the hell-fire warnings of his visiting preacher-uncles, began to develop a decidedly secular point of view. In the summers he helped Townley Crane gather news and gossip for his *Tribune* column, "On the Jersey Coast." By 1888, when he enrolled at Claverack College and Hudson River Institute, a quasi-military prep school at Claverack, New York, he was already in full revolt against his Methodist heritage. As one of his classmates reported, he was bohemian in dress and manner, aloof and taciturn except on the baseball field, where he was companionable and "giftedly profane." . . .

Becoming a Journalist

His single year of higher education, at two different colleges, was notably unsuccessful. At Lafayette College, where he enrolled in the fall of 1890, he played baseball and delivered self-assured literary opinions—Tolstoy, whose novel of the Crimean War, *Sebastopol* (1855), he had read, was the world's greatest writer; [Gustave] Flaubert's *Salammbô* (1862) was too long; Henry James's *The Reverberator* (1888) was a bore—but he did no work, and at the end of the term was advised to withdraw. At Syracuse University for the spring semester of 1891, he haunted the baseball diamond and, as a part-time reporter for the *Tribune*, scouted the Syracuse tenderloin and police court, studying "humanity," as he explained, rather than the "cut and dried" lessons of the classroom. . . .

At Asbury Park he apparently took charge of Townley Crane's *Tribune* column in the summers of 1891 and 1892, gathering news and gossip at the resort hotels, recording events at the Methodist religious conferences at nearby Ocean Grove, and reporting on the annual seminars in the arts and sciences at another neighboring community, Avon-by-the-Sea. During this time he was also working out a theory of art, evidently basing it partly on theories of realism advanced by Hamlin Garland and William Dean Howells, partly on ideas expressed by the realist painter-hero of Kipling's novel *The Light That Failed* (1891), and partly on the practical demonstration of the uses of irony and the handling of psychological realism in Tolstoy's *Sebastopol*. Strolling the beach with a friend who asked his advice about writing, Crane tossed a handful of sand in the air and said, "Treat your notions like that. Forget what you think about it and tell how you feel about it." . . .

Into the Bowery

Perhaps at Garland's suggestion Crane began his firsthand study of city life in the summer of 1891, going into the Bowery [an area of New York City known at the time for its brothels, flophouses, and beer gardens] from his brother Ed's house in Lake View, New Jersey, within easy commuting distance of New York, to study the color of the city and the effect of the slums on the morals and manners of the poor. A year or so later, in August, 1892, his propensity for satire got the Crane brothers in trouble: the owner-editor of the *Tribune*, a Republican candidate that year for the vice-presidency of the United States, fired both Stephen and Townley Crane when the young satirist's graphic and ironic description of a labor-union parade in Asbury Park aroused the ire of the politically influential unionists. His ties with Asbury Park broken with the sudden demise of Townley Crane's agency, Stephen Crane now moved to the city, taking up precarious residence in the semi-bohemian quarters of aspiring actors, medical students, and commercial illustrators and beginning his study of tenement life in earnest. He disappeared for days into the Bowery disguised as a derelict, gathering material for sketches and newspaper stories, which he occasionally sold to the *Herald*, and perhaps for his novel *Maggie*, begun either at Syracuse in the spring of 1891 or, more likely, in the late fall after his first excursions into the city. He revised the novel in March 1892 and showed it to Richard Watson Gilder, the editor of the *Century* magazine, who thought it "cruel" and "too honest" in its description of the sordid life of the slums. Crane revised it again that winter, but after it was rejected by editor after editor, Crane gave up. Borrowing money from his brother Will and raising some on the coal-mine stock he inherited from his father, he had the novel privately printed. It appeared in February or March 1893 under the pseudonym Johnston Smith, an ugly, yellow, little book no bookstore would take, except Brentano's, which stocked twelve copies and returned ten. . . .

During the years 1893 and 1894, when he was reworking *Maggie* and writing *The Red Badge of Courage* . . . , Crane continued, apparently by choice, to live in wretched poverty, convinced that suffering was beneficial to his art. This conviction he probably owed to Kipling's *The Light That Failed*, which he most likely read as early as 1891 and which apparently exerted considerable influence on his literary ideas. The hero of the novel, a realist painter who theorizes a good deal about realistic art, advocates poverty as a spur to creativity. "There are few things more edifying unto Art," he says, "than the belly-pinch of hunger," an idea Crane echoed later when he stated that the fact that *The Red Badge of Courage* was "an effort born of pain, despair, almost" made it "a better piece of literature than it otherwise would have been." Seeking first-hand experience of the bitter life of the poor, he lived in a gloomy, rundown, ill-heated old building, often as cold and hungry as the derelicts he studied in the Bowery. . . .

Writing *The Red Badge*

But he also wrote during this time, beginning in March or April of 1893, *The Red Badge of Courage*, the novel of the Civil War which made him famous when it was published in 1895 and which has long been regarded as one of the classics of American literature. Unlike *Maggie* . . . , which seem to honor a basic tenet of his theory of realism—namely, that truth in art is grounded in actual observation and experience—*The Red Badge of Courage* was apparently a pure invention, written years before its author ever actually saw a battle. But in an important sense real-life experience probably contributed little more to *Maggie* than to the war novel, for although he doubtless observed in the slums most of the particulars of *Maggie*, Crane appropriated the major elements of the novel from the myth of the slum girl, a myth readily accessible in the popular literature of the time—in Edgar Fawcett's *The Evil That Men Do* (1889) and in articles about slum life in the *Arena* magazine, for example. In these writings he found the character types (the pure, betrayed slum girl, the drunken parents, the vicious brother), the attitudes (the scorn of hypocritical respectability, the veneration of purity in women), actions (the fights, the seduction, the suicide of the heroine), and ideas (the powers of vanity and social forces)—all elements which he incorporated in the plot of *Maggie*. *The Red Badge of Courage* apparently originated in much the same way, deriving similarly from a popular myth of war. As Stanley Wertheim has shown, the numerous memoirs of war veterans which appeared in the 1860s, 1870s, and 1880s had established by 1890 "a distinctive literary convention for Civil War narratives, embodied in literally dozens of exemplars," many of which Crane, with his lifelong obsession with war, must have known. He obviously drew upon the common pattern of these chronicles for the major elements of plot in *The Red Badge of Courage*: the sentimental expectation of the young recruit moved to enlist by patriotic rhetoric and heroic fantasies of war, the resistance of his parents to his enlistment, his anxiety over the apparent confusion and purposelessness of troop movements, his doubts about his personal courage, the dissipation of his heroic illusions in his first battle, his grumbling about the incompetency of generals, and other such motifs, incidents, and situations. H.T. Webster has demonstrated that 'everything [except style and execution] that makes up *The Red Badge of Courage* exists at least in germ" in Wilbur Hinman's *Corporal Si Klegg and His Pard* (1887), a story about a raw recruit who, like Crane's Henry Fleming, is given to romantic self-dramatization and anxious worry about his personal courage but who eventually proves himself in battle and is praised for heroism by his colonel.

Forces That Shaped the Novel

It is style and execution directed by a powerful imagination which transmutes these commonplace narrative conventions into literature; in a sense, the literary method and the ideas Crane developed in his *Tribune* pieces and New York writings are more relevant to the question of origins than any of these historical accounts. He probably developed his method chiefly on the model of Tolstoy's ironic, impressionistic *Sebastopol*, which demonstrates the powerful dramatic effect of representing reality in the imagery of the hero's psychological life. He may have found in Kipling's *The Light That Failed* an adaptable illustration of the dramatic use of color, as his repetitive use of Kipling's wrathful red-sun image in *The Red Badge of Courage* and other works suggests. The style he shaped from these models was validated theoretically by Howells's concept of realism as the truthful treatment of materials and by Garland's idea that truth is the artist's subjective view of it. Thus when Crane turned to his imaginary war in the spring of 1893, he was in command of formidable literary resources: the plot elements provided by the conventionalized Civil War story, an attitude toward it sanctioned by contemporary theories of realism, a literary character developed in his studies of the little man in his Asbury Park and Sullivan County pieces, and a vivid impressionistic style inspired by Tolstoy and Kipling.

Another force at work in the shaping of the novel was the effect on Crane's imagination of his intense preoccupation at this time with religious questions, the explicit evidence for which is in his book of poems, *The Black Riders*. More than half of the sixty-eight poems of the volume are on religious themes—the inscrutability of God, man's futile quest for God, God's wrath, the terrors of a Godless universe, and man's pride and impotence—which express Crane's anguished uncertainty about God's character and man's relation to him. Is God dead and man abandoned to an indifferent universe, the questioning runs, or is he, on the contrary, terribly present in the world, a God of wrath breathing hatred and malice on helpless, sinful man? . . . The God of wrath and the God of indifference often appear in images of hostile or stolidly impassive mountains. In one poem, angry mountains appear as an army of vengeance against a defiant little man: "On the horizon the peaks assembled; / As I looked, / The march of the mountains began"; and in still another: "Once I saw mountains angry, / And ranged in battle-front. / Against them stood a little man; / Aye, he was no bigger than my finger." And yet another man, "clambering to the house-tops" to appeal to the heavens, finds God, at last, in "the sky . . . filled with armies."

The Little Man Alone Against Nature

The recurrent motif of the little man against the hostile mountain first appears in expanded form as one of the 1892 Sullivan County stories, "The Mesmeric Mountain," a fablelike narrative of the little man's war against nature which not only outlines the plot of *The Red Badge of Courage* but also explains the symbolic meaning of the motif in the novel, where it occurs a number of times at crucial points in the narrative. The hero of the fable is the little man, who, contemplating the "ecstatic mystery" of a road leading into a pine forest, decides to follow it, certain that "it leads to something great or something." Making his way through the forest, battling "hordes of ignorant bushes" and "obstructing branches," he pauses at sundown to rest near the foot of a mountain. Gazing idly at the mountain in the fading light of "the red silence" of the sinking sun and the "formidable" shadows of the pines, he suddenly perceives that the mountain has eyes and is watching him. It appears about to attack, and the little man springs to his feet and flees in terror. Later, he pauses and, returning cautiously, is horrified to see that the mountain "has followed him" and is now about to crush his head with its heel. In a blind rage, he attacks, flinging pebbles against its face and scrambling wildly up toward its summit, which he perceives as "a blaze of red wrath." when he reaches the top at last, he thrusts his hands "scornfully in his pockets" and swaggers victoriously about, confidently identifying distant landmarks. He does not notice that "the mountain under his feet was motionless."

Nearly all of the elements of the war novel are in the fable. Like Henry Fleming in *The Red Badge of Courage*, the little man is motivated to his adventure by heroic expectations of "great things," and like Henry's mother, the little man's camping companion disapproves of the undertaking. Both heroes project their anxieties on the landscape, animating it in their morbid fancies with menacing life. Both are obliged to force their ways against an unfriendly nature, "ignorant bushes" and "obstructing branches." Both are terrorized by perceptions of hostile supernatural forces which seem to threaten their destruction, and both are driven in desperation to attack them. Finally, both entertain illusions of victory and celebrate their delusive triumphs in secret ceremonies of self-congratulation.

The prominence of the imagery of menace and threat in the landscape in *The Red Badge of Courage*, particularly in the images of mountains and hills, clearly shows that the novel, the fable, and the poems all have a common origin in Crane's imagination. Although the novel enlarges the metaphor of the angry mountain to include nature in general, the mountain is nevertheless a central symbol. A passage in chapter 17 describes Henry's reaction when his lieutenant praises him for his violent assault against the attacking enemy: "He had been a tremendous figure, no doubt," Henry thinks complacently. "By this struggle he had overcome obstacles which he had admitted to be mountains. They had fallen like paper peaks, and he was now what he called a hero." Obviously, Henry is symbolically identical with the vainglorious hero of the fable who struts like a victor on the peak of the motionless mountain.

The passage suggests that Henry from the beginning has been as much concerned about how he measures up to nature—and, by extension, to God—as he has about how he measures up to war. For in his imagination, the terror of war—"the blood-swollen god"—and the terror of nature become one. Mountains, fields, streams, the night, the sun, appear in his disordered fancy in guises of living creatures, monstrous and terrible.

Yielding to Larger Purposes

But the meaning of the landscape shifts with Henry's moods and fortunes: his fear is its hostility, his complacency is its sympathy. Humiliated by his panicky flight from his first

Stephen Crane. The Library of Congress.

battle, he turns to nature for solace and comfort. Wending his way in a peaceful forest, he is gratified to observe that nature is "a woman with a deep aversion to tragedy." He reaches a secluded place where "high arching boughs made a chapel," and he supposes that tender nature has furnished it for his need

29

and convenience. He pushes the "green doors" aside and is suddenly transfixed with horror. Sitting on the "gentle brown carpet" in the "religious half-light" is a rotting corpse, an abomination in the very nave of peaceful nature. When he tries to flee, it seems to him that nature turns on him in a fury, that the snagging branches and brambles at the threshold of the delusive chapel now try to throw him on the unspeakable corpse. But at a distance, the aspect of the horrible chapel seems to change, like the enraged mountain in the fable: "The trees about the portal of the chapel moved soughingly in a soft wind. A sad silence was upon the little, guarding edifice." Earlier, after his company has beaten off an enemy attack, he has glanced upward and felt "a flash of astonishment at the blue sky and the sun gleaming on the trees and fields"; it has seemed to him "surprising that nature had gone tranquilly on with her golden processes in the midst of so much devilment." Such shifts in Henry's perception are signs of his spiritual disorder. A victim of his vain expectations, he can never be certain whether nature is hostile or sympathetic, or merely indifferent.

When Henry is returned to his regiment by the humble and competent "cheery soldier," he finds that his braggart friend Wilson, "the loud soldier," veteran now of a battle, has undergone a remarkable change: he no longer regards anxiously "the proportions of his personal prowess" but shows now a "fine reliance" and "quiet belief in his purposes and abilities." "He was no more a loud young soldier." Henry wonders "where had been born these new eyes" and notes that Wilson "apparently had now climbed a peak of wisdom from which he could perceive himself as a very wee thing." The meaning of the mountain image has clearly shifted: it is no longer the angry mountain driving an exasperated little man to desperate but futile assault, but "a peak of wisdom" from which he is able to perceive correctly his humble place in the scheme of things. Having exorcised his corrupting vanity, Wilson sees himself and the world clearly and truly, as Henry later does also after he yields himself to the larger purposes of the regiment and heroically leads a charge against the enemy.

The Warring Sides of Crane's Imagination

But the problem with Henry is different. Wilson's conversion is merely given; Henry's must, according to the narrative logic, be demonstrated. Figuratively, he is the little man at war against God as well as against the Confederate enemy, and the war against God he cannot win. When Crane describes Henry's moral transformation in the final chapter, he simply drops the issue of his hero's adversary relation to the landscape. Revising the text before submitting it to Appleton for publication, he deleted in the last chapter all crucial reference to Henry's experience with nature. He struck the sentence "Echoes of his terrible combat with the arrayed forces of the universe came to his ears," and he struck also Henry's thought that the God of wrath could have justly commanded his obeisance—"that he had been wrong not to kiss the knife and bow to the cudgel." He deleted references to the indifference of nature and to Henry's momentary impulse to see himself "once again fraternizing with nature," remembering presumably the harmony he felt with it in the forest before finding the corpse in the little chapel-like bower. Crane deleted also Henry's reflection that he could "no more stand upon places high and false, and denounce the distant planets." As these cancellations suggest, Crane's attitude toward God was markedly ambivalent, as it is in *The Black Riders*, and his purpose in the revision was apparently to avoid the problem of resolving the whole uncertain issue of Henry's war against God. This evasion is undoubtedly the reason for the diminished vitality of the chapters describing Henry's heroic battlefield exploits: the slackness of the irony, as in the notoriously sentimental description of Henry's feeling about the rescued flag, and the weakening of the symbolic resonance of the imagery.

The irreconcilable tension between Crane's religious and heroic imaginations is clearly revealed in this weakness in construction. If the second half of the novel is much like the conventional heroic war story (expressive certainly of one side of Crane's nature), the first half is powerfully and originally imaginative. The pathos of Henry's alienation in an incomprehensible world, of his helplessness under the spell of his vanity, and of his poignant yearnings for a sign is brilliantly rendered. Generations of readers have found memorable the fantastic descriptions of the landscape, the gay humor of the country maiden's heroic battle to rescue her cow from the fat thieving soldier, the horror of the discovery in the little forest chapel, the awesome death of Jim Conklin, the patient and selfless suffering of "the tattered man," the manliness of the anonymous "cheery soldier," and other scenes, incidents, and characters.

Publishing *The Red Badge*

The first publication of *The Red Badge of Courage*, like that of *Maggie*, was irregular and discouraging. *McClure's Monthly* accepted it, presumably intending to publish it as a serial. But after six months of waiting, Crane, doubtful that any such plan would ever be carried out, withdrew it and sold it for ninety dollars to Irving Bacheller, who carved away two-thirds of the text and distributed this abridged version to his newspaper syndicate. It appeared in the *Philadelphia Press*, the *New York Press*, and many other newspapers across the nation (in serial form in many) in early December 1894. Pleased by the favorable response of editors and readers and impressed by Crane's demonstrated powers of description, Bacheller engaged him as a special correspondent and ordered him on a journalistic expedition to Mexico via Nebraska, Louisiana, Arkansas, and Texas. Hastily completing arrangements for the publication of *The Black Riders*, which an editor friend had recommended to a Boston publisher of experimental poetry, and of *The Red Badge of Courage*, the newspaper version of which had attracted the attention of the publisher D. Appleton, Crane departed on his four months' journey west in late January 1895. . . .

When he returned to New York City in mid-May 1895, he paused to distribute signed copies of *The Black Riders*, which had appeared a few days before his arrival, and then went west to his brother Edmund's house in Hartwood, in Sullivan County, where he lived, with frequent sojourns in the city and other places, for more than a year. . . .

A Discontented Realist

As his letters of late 1895 and early 1896 suggest, his literary situation was somewhat problematic, paradoxically because of the immense success of *The Red Badge of Courage*. It created something of a sensation in late 1895, and before the end of that year Crane was a famous man, an international celebrity known on both sides of the Atlantic for his brilliant and uncompromisingly realistic portrayal of war. But the novel seemed to prove that he was more a realist in theory than in practice, and he was painfully aware that his literary mentors, Howells and Garland, would take it as clear evidence of his abandonment of serious literary purpose, a view Howells more than hinted when he wrote Crane early in 1896: "For me, I remain true to my first love, 'Maggie.' That is better than all the Black Riders and Red Badges." Crane had anticipated the point, however, for in November 1895, about the time he was expressing surprise at his sudden fame and reporting that his incoming mail at Hartwood had "reached mighty proportions," he felt obliged to reaffirm his program as a literary realist: "I decided [in 1892], " he wrote an editor, "that the nearer a writer gets to life, the greater he becomes as an artist, and most of my prose writings have been toward the goal partially described by that misunderstood and abused word, realism." He complained about the war novel, as if he blamed it

for the predicament it had put him in by making him an authority on war, which he had never seen, and by establishing
him as a master of realism, whose first principle he had conspicuously violated. He began in those early months of his
fame to derogate the novel: "I suppose I ought to be thankful
to 'The Red Badge' but I am much fonder of my little book of
poems, 'The Black Riders.' My aim was to comprehend in it
the thoughts I have had about life in general, while 'The Red
Badge' is a mere episode in life, an amplification" (a comment
which may suggest, incidentally, that he was conscious of a
significant relationship in the themes of the two books). And
he referred to it variously as the "damned 'Red Badge,'" "that
damned book," "the accursed 'Red Badge.'"

A Writer Testing His Own Courage

Ken Chowder

Prize-winning documentary film writer Ken Chowder has scripted more than twenty projects, including several documentaries for PBS and National Geographic. He has written articles about history, literature, sports, and science for Smithsonian, American Heritage, *and other major periodicals.*

In the following viewpoint, Chowder states that although Stephen Crane was born after the American Civil War, his depiction of a soldier's experiences during that war seemed uncannily real to contemporary readers of The Red Badge of Courage. *As if to live up to the gritty and masculine lifestyle of the soldiers he wrote of in that novel, Crane was driven to display his own courage and adventurous spirit by becoming a newspaper war correspondent in late nineteenth-century conflicts, Chowder writes. Crane tried, but failed, to cover the revolution in Cuba in 1897 and then was quickly sent to report on the Greco-Turkish War. Upon his return to the States a year later, he set off immediately to Cuba to cover U.S. action there during the Spanish-American War. Chowder states that according to eyewitnesses, Crane stood bravely through the battle of San Juan Hill as bullets struck all about him. In Chowder's view, such foolhardiness may have been Crane's attempt to die in battle—a wish he had imparted to friends once he had become aware that a less-than-glorious death at the hands of tuberculosis would likely be his fate.*

Ken Chowder, "A Writer Who Lived the Adventures He Portrayed," *Smithsonian*, vol. 45, no. 10, January 1995, pp. 109–121. Copyright © Smithsonian Magazine. Reproduced by permission of the author.

Because of its gritty realism, impressionistic style and icono-clastic views, *The Red Badge of Courage* was nothing less than revolutionary. It was the first popular American novel to question the romance and glory of war. Its hero, Henry Fleming, is "jest one little feller" in an anonymous war of mud and confusion. Henry had "dreamed of battles all his life—of vague and bloody conflicts that had thrilled him with their sweep and fire. . . . He had imagined peoples secure in the shadow of his eagle-eyed prowess." But Henry is a very human "little feller": he runs at the first serious sniff of battle, displaying the "zeal of an insane sprinter." Then he rationalizes his flight: "He had done a good part in saving himself, who was a little piece of the army. . . . His actions had been sagacious things. They had been full of strategy. They were the work of a master's legs." Later he repents, and wishes he had a wound, "a red badge of courage." He gets his wish, but with Crane's typical ironic twist: the "red badge" comes from being clubbed in the head by his own comrade.

When Henry watches ants crawl over the face of a soldier's decaying corpse, the patriotic veil is lifted from the face of war. This is why the book revolted the old guard of the military. A former general blasted it, writing that the hero "is an ignorant and stupid country lad . . . without a spark of patriotic feeling or even of soldierly ambition." Henry "is throughout an idiot or a maniac," the outraged general wrote. "No thrill of patriotic devotion . . . moves his breast, and not even an emotion of manly courage."

War from a New Point of View

It is a mistake to see *The Red Badge* as being simply antiwar. Later Crane would write, "war is neither magnificent nor squalid; it is simply life." But it is intensified life, complete with stupidity and evil; courage, for Crane, is a magnificent thing all the same—absurd, yet magnificent.

And Henry does show courage: he returns to his unit and fights. There is certainly an ironic touch in the book's ending, when Henry imagines "an existence of soft and eternal peace," but Henry has felt both fear and courage. He has lived; "he was a man."

The Red Badge is written with a powerful economy and intensity that has variously been called "poetic," "symbolist," "impressionistic," "realistic" and "naturalistic." Even its language seemed new, and still does—a dead man's eyes are the "dull hue to be seen on the side of a dead fish"; of another man he said, "there was a great uncertainty about his knee joints"; a wounded man "had a shoeful of blood. He hopped like a schoolboy in a game."

The Red Badge of Courage was the zenith of Stephen Crane's writing career. It was first published in serial form by hundreds of newspapers; the book itself came out to what [British novelist] H. G. Wells called an "orgy of praise." "At times the description of battle is so vivid as to be almost suffocating," the *New York Press* wrote. "This is war from a new point of view. . . . One should be forever slow in calling an author a genius, but . . . *The Red Badge of Courage* [has] greater power and originality than can be girdled by the name of talent." The novel was a best-seller here and in England. In one year it went through 14 printings.

The Road to Oblivion

But even at this high point, the beginning of his fame, there was something ominous in Crane—as if his fate were already written on his dark, serious face. Early in 1895, he went West to do a little reporting and "get rid of his cough," according to the young [American novelist] Willa Cather, whom he met in Nebraska. Crane seemed to be "brooding over some impending disaster," Cather said. His eyes "seemed to be burning themselves out." As she later wrote, "Now that he is dead it occurs to me that all his life was a preparation for sudden departure." There was a strongly morbid streak in the young and sickly writer. After he visited the death chamber at Sing Sing [Prison in New York], he wrote: "It is a fine short road to oblivion." The line could serve as his epitaph.

Crane went South from Nebraska to New Orleans, Galveston, San Antonio. He took the train to Mexico City, then headed into the badlands on horseback, where—in true Crane fashion—he was chased into the wilderness by a gang of bandits and saved by a detachment of rurales. He spent a month in southern Mexico: "There was nothing American about me save a large Smith and Wesson revolver."

The young author was a budding celebrity, and his life, as if to match his fame, began to turn into a series of melodramas and strange incidents—instigated, some have suggested, by Crane himself. Most of the spectacularly theatrical events of his life had one thing in common. In each of them, Crane was engaged in fierce struggle—against the police, the press and standards of public morality; against the cruel sea, enemy bullets and incurable disease; against violence, nature and death. In each of them, he was testing his own courage. In that sense, the rest of his life was an extension of *The Red Badge of Courage*. . . .

The *Commodore* Shipwreck

When Crane began his active pursuit of war—and any war would do—Cuba was in revolt against Spain, so he went to Florida to find a boat to take him to Cuba. In Jacksonville he met Cora Stewart Taylor, the golden-haired (if somewhat dumpy) owner of a club called Hotel de Dream.

Cora Taylor came from a "respectable" family in Boston, had traveled extensively and was as deliberately bohemian as Crane himself. At that time, a "nightclub" usually involved prostitution, and Cora had some 12 to 15 girls at the Hotel de Dream. (A list of Jacksonville's brothels gave it a "Class A" rating.) Cora, six years older than Stephen, was an escapee from a failed marriage; her husband refused a divorce. She was impressed by the famous 25-year-old writer. Cora "seemed to know at once that writing was her true profession," according to Crane biographer R. W. Stallman, "and that author Crane was her salvation . . . here to rescue her tarnished soul from that sordid castle of false dreams."

But Crane was off to Cuba—or so he thought. He signed on as a seaman for the steamer *Commodore*, bound for Cuba with a cargo of guns. The ship hit a sandbar less than two miles out from Jacksonville and began to take on water. Having written about shipwrecks, Crane now seemed to relish the situation. The *Commodore*'s cook told a correspondent, "That newspaper feller was a nervy man. He didn't seem to know what fear was."

Crane was among the last off the ship, joining four men in an open dinghy. When one of the other lifeboats foundered, its occupants returned to the sinking *Commodore*. Crane watched as one of those seven doomed sailors simply jumped into the sea. "I could see . . . in the very toss of his head, as he leaped thus to death, that it was rage, rage, rage unspeakable that was in his heart."

Crane's dinghy tossed in the ocean for some 30 hours. In the months to come, he would base "The Open Boat," one of the great short stories in American literature, on that ordeal. In real life, as well as fiction, the captain ran the dinghy through the high waves toward the beach. It capsized and probably struck Higgins, the oiler, who perished in the surf. "In the shallows, face downward, lay the oiler," Crane wrote. "His forehead touched sand that was periodically, between each wave, clear of the sea."

Bravery as a War Journalist

Crane, still itching to know the taste of war, set sail a few months later for Greece, and the adventurous Cora followed him. Why Greece? Crane had heard that Greece and Turkey were about to fight over the independence of Crete. Like his imaginary Henry Fleming, Crane too dreamed of godlike heroism. "I shall try like blazes to get a decoration out of the thing," he wrote his brother. And it turned out he'd been right about the dual nature of war, its combination of grace and horror too. "The roll of musketry-fire . . . had the wonder of human tragedy in it. It was the most beautiful sound of my experience." The sound of a man being wounded included the "silken, sliding, tender noise of the bullet, and the thud of its impact."

But it was not much of a war: a month of half-hearted defensive actions. Cora's presence hampered Crane, and he saw only one battle. An armistice was signed, and then Crane and Cora moved to England, where they set up housekeeping as apparent husband and wife.

They lived in a large brick villa called Ravensbrook. Crane made friends with a few local writers, including Joseph Conrad, Henry James, H. G. Wells and Ford Madox Ford. The extravagant couple gave the impression of easy wealth—entertaining lavishly, buying a piano, horse, typewriter and newfangled Kodak—while knee-deep in debt. No doubt Crane seemed a bit out of place in a London suburb; at times he would entertain guests while dressed in cowboy pants, wagging a revolver in his hand. In England he wrote stories of the American West (including the classics "The Blue Hotel" and "The Bride Comes to Yellow Sky") and looked for a way out.

Then the long-simmering feud over Cuba appeared about ready to boil over and Conrad helped Crane raise enough money to get there. When the United States declared war against Spain in the spring of 1898, Crane tried to sign on as a sailor. He flunked the physical but several days later, as a highly paid correspondent, he was aboard a battleship that was shelling the city of Cabanas. Soon he was under enemy fire at Guantanamo, Las Guasimas, Cuzco and San Juan Hill—a real war at last!

So what was it like? Much like his fictional one, of course. Certainly not, as the public believed, a simple matter of flags and bright banners. As Crane watched the Army push toward Santiago, he wrote, "There wasn't a high heroic face among them; they were all men intent on business. That was all."

Cuba was a grungy war, a torture of insufferable heat, malaria and yellow fever. After only four weeks, three-quarters of Teddy Roosevelt's Rough Riders were too sick to fight. "Regulars Get No Glory" read the title of one Crane newspaper piece. When he watched the victorious landing at Daiquiri, he described what that historic occasion meant for the average soldier: it was only "an itch on his shin, a pain in his hand, hunger, thirst, a lack of sleep; the influence of his memory of past firesides, glasses of beer, girls, theaters, ideals, religions, parents, faces, hurts, joys." Another time, Crane wrote of a soldier who was "dying near me. He was dying hard. Hard. It took him a long time to die. . . . But he was going to break. He was going to break."

But if real war was horrible, it was, like the one Crane had imagined, superb as well—or men were, at least. Courageous men were. "I feel that things were often sublime," he wrote. "But . . . they were not of our shallow and preposterous fictions. . . . It was the behavior of men on the street. It was the behavior of men."

Crane himself was one of those courageous men. On one occasion, as bullets whistled by, he calmly sent signal messages by lantern to American ships. On another, he wore a gleaming white raincoat as he went up San Juan Hill. He stood atop one hill, hands in pockets, puffing a pipe until one bullet knocked off his hat and another chipped the case of his field glasses. He hauled guns and supplies for the troops during one battle; in another, he carried wounded men to the rear. Astonishing accounts of his reckless bravery under fire are abundant. To the awed correspondents around him, he simply seemed without fear, but that was not true. When he went out on reconnaissance, he said, he acted "as jaunty as a real soldier, while all the time my heart was in my boots." On another occasion, "I was frightened almost to convulsions." And again, "all that night I was afraid. Bitterly afraid."

If he was so afraid, how could he show such courage? The simplest explanation might be the best: he probably wanted to get himself killed. He told a friend that his fondest desire was to die in battle. By now he almost certainly knew he had tuberculosis and understood what that meant; TB, of course, was still considered incurable. "He looked like a frayed white ribbon," one reporter wrote.

Crane's Last Days

When he finally returned to England, early in 1899, Cora had a "new" house waiting for him. It had a huge, dank, bat-infested, 500-year-old Sussex mansion called Brede Manor, with no heat except by open fire, no water, no toilets. Another thing awaited him in England—a crushing load of debt. And one last matter: his own death.

Not long after Christmas that same year, Brede Manor was home to a house party. The festivities lasted three days; some 40 guests ate some 40 plum puddings, watched a devised play called "The Ghost," raced on broomsticks around the great hall, and danced until 2 A.M. to music from a live orchestra. At the end the host sat strumming his guitar, fainted against a guest—and then coughed up blood. His lungs had hemorrhaged. H. G. Wells bicycled seven miles in the drizzling dawn to fetch a doctor. Newspapers on both sides of the Atlantic reported the news: Stephen Crane's last days had begun.

Cora was not prepared to believe it. "The lung trouble seems to be over!" she wrote in April. She was still blindly absorbed in restoring Brede Manor. In late May they dragged Crane to a sanatorium in Germany's Black Forest, but he was long past hope. In his feverish dreams he thought he was, again, in an open boat on the indifferent sea.

"For my own part, I am minded to die in my 35th year," Crane had written at 24, after an unhappy affair. "I think that is all I care to stand." As it turned out, he did not have to stand even that much. When he passed away on June 5, 1900, he was nearly seven years shy of his goal. "What a brutal, needless extinction—what an unmitigated, unredeemed catastrophe!" Henry James lamented. But as Crane himself once said, "one makes room in Heaven for all sorts of souls . . . who are not confidently expected to be there by many excellent people."

Social Issues in Literature

CHAPTER 2

The Red Badge of Courage and War

Henry Fleming
at Chancellorsville

Harold Hungerford

Harold Hungerford was a literature professor who taught at the University of California at Berkeley as well as at Cornell University. His 1963 article on the factual framework of The Red Badge of Courage *is well known among Crane scholars.*

In The Red Badge of Courage, *Stephen Crane did not name the battle in which his main character, Henry Fleming, received his infamous wound; however, Hungerford argues in the following viewpoint, clues regarding the date, the movement of the armies, and the geography of the battlefield suggest strongly that Fleming's story takes place at Chancellorsville, Virginia. It was there, during a six-day struggle in 1863, that the Confederate army under General Robert E. Lee bested Union troops led by General Joseph Hooker. Besides the evidence given in the novel, a subsequent short story about Henry Fleming clearly indicates that Crane had situated his earlier work at that terrible battleground.*

The name of the battle in which Henry Fleming achieved his manhood is never given in *The Red Badge of Courage.* Scholars have not agreed that the battle even ought to have a name; some have implied that it is a potpourri of episodes from a number of battles. Yet an examination of the evidence leads to the conclusion that the battle does have a name—Chancellorsville. Throughout the book, it can be demonstrated, Crane consistently used the time, the place, and the actions of Chancellorsville as a factual framework within which to represent the perplexities of his young hero.

Harold Hungerford, "'That Was at Chancellorsville': The Factual Framework of *The Red Badge of Courage*," *American Literature*, vol. 34, no. 4, January 1963, pp. 520ff. Copyright © 1963, Duke University Press. Copyright renewed 1991 by Duke University Press. All rights reserved. Used by permission of the publisher.

Evidence Points to Chancellorsville

Evidence of two sorts makes the initial hypothesis that Crane used Chancellorsville probable. In the first place, Crane said so in his short story "The Veteran," which was published less than a year after *The Red Badge*. In this story he represented an elderly Henry Fleming as telling about his fear and flight in his first battle. "That was at Chancellorsville," Henry said. His brief account is consistent in every respect with the more extended account in *The Red Badge*; old Henry's motives for flight were those of the young Henry, and he referred to Jim Conklin in a way which made it clear that Jim was long since dead.

This brief reference in "The Veteran" is, so far as I know, the only direct indication Crane ever gave that the battle in *The Red Badge* was Chancellorsville. He appears never to have mentioned the matter in his letters, and his biographers recount no references to it. Such evidence as that cited above must be used with discretion; Crane might conceivably have changed his mind. But there is no good reason why he should have done so; and in any case, the clue given us by "The Veteran" can be thoroughly corroborated by a second kind of evidence, that of time and place.

No one questions that *The Red Badge* is about the Civil War; the references to Yanks and Johnnies, to blue uniforms on one side and to gray and butternut on the other clearly establish this fact. If we turn now to military history, we find that the evidence of place and time points directly to Chancellorsville.

Only three actual place-names are used in the book: Washington, Richmond, and the Rappahannock River. Henry Fleming and his fellow-soldiers had come through Washington to their winter quarters near the Rappahannock River, and their army was close enough to Richmond that cavalry could move against that city. Such a combination points to northern Virginia, through which the Rappahannock flows, to which Union soldiers would come through Washington, and from which Richmond would be readily accessible. Chancellorsville was fought in northern Virginia.

Furthermore, the battle was the first major engagement of the year, occurring when the spring rains were nearly over. The year cannot be 1861; the war began in April, and soldiers would not have spent the winter in camp. Nor can it be 1862; the first eastern battle of 1862, part of [Union general George B.] McClellan's Peninsular Campaign, in no way resembled that in the book and was far removed from the Rappahannock. It cannot be 1864; the Battle of the Wilderness was fought near the Rappahannock but did not end in a Union defeat. Its strategy was in any case significantly different from that of the battle in *The Red Badge*. Finally, 1865 is ruled out; [Confederate general Robert E.] Lee had surrendered by the time the spring rains ended.

If we are to select any actual conflict at all, a *reductio ad absurdum* ["reduction to the absurd"] indicates the first eastern battle of 1863, and that battle was Chancellorsville. Moreover, 1863 marked the turning-point in the Union fortunes; before Gettysburg the South had, as Wilson remarked in *The Red Badge*, licked the North "about every clip". After Gettysburg no Union soldier would have been likely to make such a statement; and Gettysburg was the next major battle after Chancellorsville.

Like the evidence of "The Veteran," the evidence of time and place points to Chancellorsville, and it is therefore at least a tenable hypothesis that Chancellorsville and *The Red Badge* are closely connected. In the next three sections I shall present independent proof of that hypothesis by showing that the battle in Crane's novel is closely and continuously parallel to the historical Chancellorsville.

At Winters Quarters

The events preceding the battle occupy the first two chapters and part of the third. The opening chapter establishes the situation of the Union army. As winter passed into spring, that army was resting in winter camp across a river from a Confederate army. It had been there for some time—long enough for soldiers to build huts with chimneys, long enough for a new recruit to have been encamped for some months without seeing action. " . . . there had come months of monotonous life in a camp. . . . Since his regiment had come to the field the army had done little but sit still and try to keep warm". Such was the situation of the Army of the Potomac in April, 1863; it had spent a cold, wet winter encamped at Falmouth, Virginia, on the north bank of the Rappahannock River opposite the Confederate army. The army had been inactive since mid-December; its men had dug themselves into just such huts, covered with folded tents and furnished with clay chimneys, as Crane describes. Furthermore, the arrival of a new Union commander, General Joseph Hooker, had meant hour after hour of drill and review for the soldiers; and Henry was "drilled and drilled and reviewed, and drilled and drilled and reviewed".

To this monotony the "tall soldier"—Jim Conklin— brought the news that "the cavalry started this morning. . . . They say there ain't hardly any cavalry left in camp. They're going to Richmond, or some place, while we fight all the Johnnies. It's some dodge like that". He had earlier announced, "We're goin' t' move t'-morrah—sure. . . . We're goin' 'way up th' river, cut across, an' come around in behint 'em". Of course Jim was "the fast-flying messenger of a mistake," but the mistake was solely one of dates; the infantry did not move at once. Many soldiers at Falmouth jumped to Jim's conclusion when eleven thousand cavalrymen left camp April 13 for a raid on the Confederate railroad lines near Richmond. No one in the book denied that the cavalry had left; and Jim's analysis of the flank movement was to be confirmed at the end of the book when another soldier said, "Didn't I tell yeh we'd come aroun' in behint 'em? Didn't I tell yeh so?". The strategy Jim had predicted was precisely that of Chancellorsville.

The March from Falmouth

The Union army at Falmouth did not leave camp for two weeks after the departure of the cavalry, and such a period accords with the time represented in the book; "for days" after the cavalry left, Henry fretted about whether or not he would run.

Finally Henry's regiment, the 304th New York, was assembled, and it began to march before dawn. When the sun rose, "the river was not in view". Since the rising sun was at the backs of the marching men, they were going west. The eager soldiers "expressed commiseration for that part of the army which had been left upon the river bank". That night the regiment encamped; tents were pitched and fires lighted. "When another night came", the men crossed a river on *two* pontoon bridges and continued unmolested to a camping place.

This description fits aptly the march of the Second Corps. Many of its regiments were mustered before dawn on April 28, and then marched west and away from the Rappahannock. The Second, unlike the other corps marching to Chancellorsville, was ordered not to make any special secret of its whereabouts and was allowed fires when it camped. The Second crossed the Rappahannock on *two* pontoon bridges the evening of April 30 and camped safely near Chancellorsville that night; all the other corps had to ford at least one river, without the convenience of bridges. Furthermore, by no means all of the army moved at once; two full corps and one division of the Second Corps were left behind at Falmouth to conduct a holding action against Lee.

It is clear from the text that at least one day intervened between the evening on which Henry's regiment crossed the bridges and the morning of its first day of fighting. If Crane was following the chronology of Chancellorsville, this intervening day of pensive rest was May 1, on which only the Fifth and Twelfth Corps saw fighting.

Fleming at the Center of the Union Line

Action began early for Henry's regiment the next day, the events of which parallel those at Chancellorsville on May 2. The statements about what Henry and his regiment did are clear enough. He was rudely awakened at dawn, ran down a wood road, and crossed a little stream. His regiment was moved three times before the noon meal, and then moved again; one of these movements took Henry and his companions back, for in the afternoon they proceeded over the same ground they had taken that morning and then into new territory. By early afternoon, then, Henry had seen no fighting. At last a brigade ahead of them went into action; it was routed and fled, leaving the reserves, of which Henry's regiment was a part, to withstand the enemy. The regiment successfully resisted the first charge, but when the enemy re-attacked, Henry fled.

It might seem that tracing the path of Henry and his regiment before his flight would not be impossible, but it has proved to be so. The regimental movements which Crane describes loosely parallel the movements of many regiments at Chancellorsville; they directly parallel the movements of none. Nevertheless, broad parallels do exist. Many regiments of the Second Corps moved southeast from Chancellorsville on May 2; many of them first encountered the enemy in midafternoon.

Furthermore, it can be demonstrated that the 304th, like the regiments of the Second Corps, was near the center of the Union line. In the first place, the "cheery man" tells Henry,

Audie Murphy as Henry Fleming in a scene from John Huston's film adaptation of The Red Badge of Courage. *Murphy, one of America's most decorated soldiers, became an actor after returning from World War II.* Hulton Archive/Getty Images.

and us, so. His testimony deserves some credence; anyone who can so unerringly find a regiment in the dark should know what he is talking about. Moreover, the conversation of the soldiers before the assault makes it clear that they were not facing the rebel right, which would have been opposite the Union left. Nor were they far to the Union right, as I shall show later.

The evidence given us by the terrain Henry crossed also points to a position at about the center of the Union line. During the morning and early afternoon he crossed several streams and passed into and out of cleared fields and dense woods. The land was gently rolling; there were occasional fences and now and then a house. Such topographical features, in 1863, characterized the area south and east of Chancellorsville itself. Further east, in the area held by the Union left, the terrain opened up and the dense second-growth forest thinned out; further west the forest was very thick indeed, with few fields or other open areas. But southeast of Chancellorsville, where the Union center was located, the land was cultivated to a degree; fields had been cleared and cut off from the forest by fences. Topography so conditioned action at Chancellorsville that every historian of the battle perforce described the terrain; if Crane knew the battle as well as I suggest he did, he must have known its topography.

Fleming's Path of Retreat

Topography also gives us our only clue to the untraceable path of Henry's flight. At one point he "found himself almost into a swamp. He was obliged to walk upon bog tufts, and watch his feet to keep from the oily water". A man fleeing west from the center of the Union line would have encountered swamps after a few miles of flight. The detail is perhaps minor, but it corroborates the path Henry had to follow to reach the place where he received his "red badge of courage." He went west, toward the Union right held by the Eleventh Corps.

Henry's flight led him to the path of the retreating wounded soldiers, among them Jim Conklin. The scene of Jim's death contains no localizing evidence, for Crane was concentrating upon the men, not their surroundings. Nevertheless, it is appropriate to Chancellorsville; the roads leading to the river were clogged with retreating Union wounded in the late afternoon of May 2. There were no ambulances near the battle lines, and many wounded men died as they walked.

The Site of Fleming's Wounding

By contrast, the scene of Henry's wound can be readily fixed. He received it in the middle of the most-discussed single action of the battle, an action which cost Stonewall Jackson his life and a major general his command, almost surely won the battle for Lee, and generated thirty-five years of acrimonious debate. Even today, to mention Chancellorsville is inevitably to bring up the rout of the Eleventh Corps.

About sunset on May 2, 1863, Stonewall Jackson's crack troops attacked the predominantly German Eleventh Corps. The Eleventh, which was on the extreme right of the Union line and far from the fighting, was taken wholly by surprise, and many soldiers turned and ran in terrified disorder. The result was near-catastrophe for the Union; now that Jackson's men had turned the flank, the path lay open for an assault on the entire unprotected rear of the Union army.

Appropriately enough for such a battle, Jackson's men were halted by one of history's more extraordinary military maneuvers. For in a battle in which hardly any cavalry were used, a small detachment of cavalrymen held Jackson's corps off long enough to enable artillery to be dragged into place and charged with canister. The cavalrymen could do so because the dense woods confined Jackson's men to the road. The small detachment was the Eighth Pennsylvania Cavalry; the time was between 6:30 and 7 P.M. Theirs was the only cavalry charge at Chancellorsville, and it became famous not only because it had saved the Union army—perhaps even the Union—but also because no two observers could agree on its details; any historian is therefore obliged to give the charge considerable attention.

All these elements fit the time and place of Henry's wounding. Night was falling fast after his long afternoon of flight; "landmarks had vanished into the gathered gloom". All about Henry "very burly men" were fleeing from the enemy. "They sometimes gabbled insanely. One huge man was asking of the sky, 'Say, where de plank road? Where de plank road?'" A popular stereotype holds that all Germans are burly, and an unsympathetic listener could regard rapidly-spoken German as "gabbling." Certainly the replacement of *th* by *d* fits the pattern of Germans; Crane's Swede in "The Veteran" also lacks *th*. These might be vulgar errors, but they identified a German pretty readily in the heyday of dialect stories. Furthermore, plank roads were rare in northern Virginia; but a plank road ran through the Union lines toward the Rappahannock.

One of these fleeing Germans hit Henry on the head; and after he received his wound, while he was still dazed, Henry saw the arrival of the cavalry and of the artillery:

> Around him he could hear the grumble of jolted cannon as the scurrying horses were lashed toward the front. . . . He turned and watched the mass of guns, men, and horses sweeping in a wide curve toward a gap in a fence. . . . Into the unspeakable jumble in the roadway way rode a squadron of cavalry. The faded yellow of their facings shone bravely. There was a mighty altercation.

As Henry fled the scene, he could hear the guns fire and the opposing infantry fire back. "There seemed to be a great ruck of men and munitions spread about in the forest and in the fields".

Every element of the scene is consistent with contemporary descriptions of the rout of the Eleventh Corps. The time is appropriate; May 2 was the first real day of battle at Chancellorsville as it was the first day for Henry. The place is appropriate; if Henry had begun the day in the Union center and then had fled west through the swamps, he would have come toward the right of the Union line, where the men of the Eleventh Corps were fleeing in rout. The conclusion is unavoidable: Crane's use of the factual framework of Chancellorsville led him to place his hero in the middle of that battle's most important single action.

The first day of battle in *The Red Badge* ended at last when the cheery man found Henry, dazed and wandering, and led him back to his regiment by complicated and untraceable paths.

The Second Day of Battle

The second day of battle, like the first, began early. Henry's regiment was sent out "to relieve a command that had lain long in some damp trenches". From these trenches could be heard the noise of skirmishers in the woods to the front and left, and the din of battle to the right was tremendous. Again, such a location fits well enough the notion of a center regiment; the din on the right, in the small hours of May 3, would have come from Jackson's men trying to re-establish their connection with the main body of Lee's army.

Soon, however, Henry's regiment was withdrawn and began to retreat from an exultant enemy; Hooker began such a withdrawal about 7:30 A.M. on May 3. Finally the retreat stopped and almost immediately thereafter Henry's regiment was sent on a suicidal charge designed to prevent the enemy from breaking the Union lines. This charge significantly resembles that of the 124th New York, a regiment raised principally in the county which contains Port Jervis, Crane's hometown; and the time of this charge of the 124th—about 8:30 A.M.—fits the time-scheme of *The Red Badge* perfectly.

The next episode can be very precisely located; Crane's description is almost photographically accurate. Henry was about a quarter of a mile south of Fairview, the "slope on the left" from which the "long row of guns, gruff and maddened, denounc[ed] the enemy". Moreover, "in the rear of this row of guns stood a house, calm and white, amid bursting shells. A congregation of horses, tied to a railing, were tugging frenziedly at their bridles. Men were running hither and thither". This is a good impression of the Chancellor House, which was used as the commanding general's headquarters and which alone, in a battle at which almost no cavalry were present, had many horses belonging to the officers and orderlies tied near it.

The second charge of the 304th, just before the general retreat was ordered, is as untraceable as the first. It has, however, its parallel at Chancellorsville: several regiments of the Second Corps were ordered to charge the enemy about 10 A.M. on May 3 to give the main body of the army time to withdraw the artillery and to begin its retreat.

The two days of battle came to an end for Henry Fleming when his regiment was ordered to "retrace its way" and rejoined first its brigade and then its division on the way back toward the river. Such a retreat, in good order and relatively free from harassment by an exhausted enemy, began at Chancellorsville about 10 A.M. on May 3. Heavy rains again were beginning to make the roads into bogs; these rains prevented the Union soldiers from actually re-crossing the river for two days, for the water was up to the level of several of the bridges. "It rained" in the penultimate paragraph of *The Red Badge*; and the battle was over for Henry Fleming as for thousands of Union soldiers at Chancellorsville.

Crane's Resources

This long recitation of parallels, I believe, demonstrates that Crane used Chancellorsville as a factual framework for his novel. We have reliable external evidence that Crane studied *Battles and Leaders of the Civil War* in preparation for *The Red Badge* because he was concerned with the accuracy of his novel. He could have found in the ninety pages *Battles and Leaders* devotes to Chancellorsville all the information he needed on strategy, tactics, and topography. A substantial part of these ninety pages is devoted to the rout of the Eleventh Corps and the charge of the Eighth Pennsylvania Cavalry. These pages also contain what someone so visually minded as Crane could hardly have overlooked: numerous illustrations, many from battlefield sketches. The illustrations depict, among other subjects, the huts at Falmouth; men marching in two parallel columns; pontoon bridges; the Chancellor House during and after the battle; and the rout of the Eleventh. With these Crane could have buttressed the unemotional but authoritative reports of Union and Confederate officers which he found in *Battles and Leaders*.

If it is unfashionable to regard Crane as a man concerned with facts, we ought to remember that late in his life he wrote *Great Battles of the World*—hack work, to be sure, but scrupulously accurate in its selection of incident and detail and in its analysis of strategy. One can do far worse than to learn about Bunker Hill from Crane.

Why Chancellorsville?

Two questions remain unanswered. First, why did Crane not identify the battle in *The Red Badge* as he did in "The Veteran"? One answer is fairly simple: no one called the battle Chancellorsville in the book because no one would have known it was Chancellorsville. No impression is more powerful to the reader of Civil War reports and memoirs than that officers and men seldom knew where they were. They did not know the names of hills, of streams, or even of villages. Probably not more than a few hundred of the 130,000 Union men at Chancellorsville knew until long afterwards the name of the four corners around which the battle raged. A private soldier knew his own experiences, but not names or strategy; we have been able to reconstruct the strategy and the name because Crane used a factual framework for his novel; and the anonymity of the battle is the result of that framework.

Of course the anonymity is part of Crane's artistic technique as well. We do not learn Henry Fleming's full name until Chapter II; we never learn Wilson's first name. Crane sought to give only so much detail as was necessary to the integrity of the book. . . .

Why, with the whole Civil War available, should Crane have chosen Chancellorsville? Surely, in the first place, because he knew a good deal about it. Perhaps he had learned from his brother, "an expert in the strategy of Gettysburg and Chancellorsville" [according to scholar Thomas Beer]. More probably he had heard old soldiers talk about their war experiences while he was growing up. Many middle-aged men in Port Jervis had served in the 124th New York; Chancellorsville had been their first battle, and first impressions are likely to be the most vivid. It is hard to believe that men in an isolated small town could have resisted telling a hero-worshiping small boy about a great adventure in their lives.

Moreover, Chancellorsville surely appealed to Crane's sense of the ironic and the colorful. The battle's great charges, its moments of heroism, went only to salvage a losing cause; the South lost the war and gained only time from Chancellorsville; the North, through an incredible series of blunders, lost a battle it had no business losing. The dead, as always, lost the most. And when the battle ended, North and South were just where they had been when it began. There is a tragic futility about Chancellorsville just as there is a tragic futility to *The Red Badge.*

Henry Fleming, the Self-Absorbed Soldier

Perry Lentz

Perry Lentz is professor emeritus of English language and litera-
ture at Kenyon College in Gambier, Ohio. He is the author of
three novels, The Falling Hills, It Must Be Now the Kingdom
Coming, *and* Perish *from the Earth, and a nonfiction title on*
The Red Badge of Courage *called* Private Fleming at Chancellorsville: "The Red Badge of Courage" in the Civil War.

In the viewpoint that follows, Lentz claims that while it might be
idealistic to assume that soldiers in battle are concerned with
righteous causes and comradeship, Stephen Crane has his char-
acter, Henry Fleming, think primarily of self-preservation and
the safeguarding of his reputation among his fighting compan-
ions. In combat, Fleming is not a model soldier, Lentz writes. He
cares little for military discipline and acts out of emotions such
as revenge and a desire to prove his manhood. Thus Fleming's
eventual heroism in battle is made ironic, Lentz argues, because
it is never motivated by patriotism or an adherence to military
training. For this reason, Lentz maintains that Crane's novel fits
comfortably with other antiwar fiction that questions blind loy-
alty and jingoism.

L et us begin with obvious things: how Crane's novel deals
with immediately familiar assumptions and perceptions
about warfare. Military service is traditionally associated with
training in certain particular, interrelated human virtues such
as discipline, or loyalty to something larger than oneself (a
nation, a cause, a unit, and so on), or—supremely—comradeship. It could be logically assumed that any private soldier

who succeeds heroically in combat would possess these virtues, that his conduct would demonstrate their worth.

Private Fleming evinces none of these. Despite all those winter months of drill and review, basic discipline—even discipline of a grudging but self-denying sort—plays no part in his constitution. On his way into battle, military discipline is a "box" completely external to himself, compelling him forward with "iron laws of tradition and law". His first act in combat is to ignore his company commander's express order not to "shoot till I tell you" and instead to fire "a first wild shot". His training has obviously not instilled sufficient discipline in him to overmaster his panic, nor does discipline compel him back to the firing line thereafter. A certain "creed of soldiers" has been impressed upon him: "His education had been that success for that mighty blue machine was certain" and he "discarded all his speculations" about the happy possibility of a Union defeat that would vindicate his conduct. Just before receiving the blow to his head, Crane says Fleming had "returned" to that "creed". But this is a "return" only in his thinking: this "creed" does nothing thereafter to discipline his own conduct.

Fleming's Vainglory

In fact each of "Those performances which had been witnessed by his fellows" and had made him a hero results from spontaneous, self absorbed, and undisciplined moments. Completely absorbed in his personal early morning combat with the rebels, he continued firing even after "there ain't anything t' shoot at", presumably even after an order to cease fire. When he joined Lieutenant Hasbrouck in trying to inspire the 304th New York as they faltered in their counterattack, it is a specifically undisciplined action (as a private soldier, his place is in the ranks, not "gyrating" in front of the regiment's colors), inspired by "a sudden unspeakable indignation against his officer". During this counterattack, finding himself near the colors, he was seized by a sudden "love," powerful but lurid, for the thing: "It was a creation of beauty and invulnerability". This is an emotion bereft of any sense of the value of the flag to his regiment. His springing to grasp it is an instinctive, boldly self-assertive action; his keeping the flag boldly to the front is a compound of his personal infatuation with the symbol and his desire for "a fine revenge upon the officer who had referred to him and his fellows as mule drivers". His final action as flag-bearer is of a piece with these others: motivated by the still-rankling damage to his own self-esteem, by thoughtless impulse, by a vainglorious desire to capture that rebel flag. None of this is to suggest that Fleming is an isolated instance in the ranks of the 304th New York Volunteer Infantry Regiment: endemic problems with its discipline appear both early and late. But note that, in his case, both his abject failures and his subsequent successes occur not because he has absorbed military discipline, but because he has not.

Willing to Sacrifice Loyalty to Self-Interest

The dearth of any concern whatsoever for the causes of the Civil War is one of the novel's most famous attributes. Private Fleming is not necessarily bereft of loyalty to the Union cause or to the cause of freedom for the slave, but if he does feel any, it never surfaces in his mind and is not significant enough to motivate him. At that instant during his first engagement when he was dimly aware he had become "not a man but a member," he was even more dimly aware of feeling loyal to something larger than "concern for himself" at this moment: "He felt that something of which he was a part—a regiment, an army, a cause, or a country—was in a crisis". His inability to define the object of his loyalty confirms that it is no such thing but, rather, a sort of back-construction. Soldiers go into combat (he assumes) because they are loyal to something greater than their own self-interest; he is in combat and is not as self-absorbed as he was; thus he must be being loyal to *something*, even if he is not sure just what it is (note the implication of the conjunction "or" in the phrase "or a country"). He is, shortly, willing to sacrifice any of these—his regiment, then his army, cause, and country—if such would assuage the wound to his self-esteem inflicted by his panicked flight. When he learned that the line from which he fled had "held 'im" after all, he cringed "as if discovered in a crime." The 304th New York became to him that "imbecile line" that held because of its "blind ignorance and stupidity." He wished instead that the regiment had been shattered, "every little piece" in it "rescuing itself if possible," because then his own flight would be vindicated. He felt "a great anger against his comrades" and "ill used". As he later watched the panic-stricken retreat of the Eleventh Corps, he was "comforted in a measure by this sight"—the sight, that is, of the single greatest catastrophe to befall a corps of the Army of the Potomac during the course of the Civil War. "There was an amount of pleasure to him in watching the wild march of this vindication". Though his thinking during these minutes did waver, "yet, he said, in a half-apologetic manner to his conscience, he could not but know that a defeat for the army this time might mean many favorable things for him". And "he said, as if in excuse for this hope, that previously the army had encountered great defeats and in a few months had shaken off all blood and tradition of them, emerging as bright and valiant as a new one; thrusting out of sight the memory of disaster, and appearing with the valor and confidence of unconquered legions".

It is at once both hilarious and appalling to see a private soldier rationalizing so readily his private "hope" that his army's present campaign would end in another "great defeat." To fulfill this "hope," Fleming "felt no compunctions for proposing a general as a sacrifice," even if the public outrage might "hit the wrong man". Although Fleming would have no way of knowing this, it was probably beyond the power of the outnumbered rebels to inflict such a "great defeat" upon the

Army of the Potomac. But had they been able to do so and had that army collapsed, more than a single general would have been sacrificed. So too, most likely, would have been the "cause" and the "country" for which it had assembled.

Vindicating His Self-Worth

In point of historical fact, for the third spring in a row, the major Federal army in the east had marched southward full of confidence only to find itself in extremely short order fighting for its very survival. To this general experience add one total defeat at the Second Battle of Bull Run, a stalemate at Antietam in the bloodiest single day in American military history, and all the utterly vain sacrifice in blundering assaults against the rebel lines at Fredericksburg the previous winter. A catastrophic disaster could now quite likely have overwhelmed the Federal army's powers of resilience: even the humiliating moral defeat that ensued all but destroyed its confidence. That the Army of the Potomac did manage to forge ahead until final victory owed a great deal to its victory later this summer at Gettysburg (a virtual gift from General R. E. Lee, accomplished after three days of severe slaughter), and even more to the institution of national conscription. The latter, though bitterly resented and opposed, refilled with drafted men divisions depleted by bloodshed, defeat, and the consequent collapse of active support for the war—the kind of support that previously had supplied hundreds of regiments of willing volunteers (such as the 304th New York) to the Union armies. Fleming finally "discarded all his speculations" in this "direction," and "returned to the creed of soldiers." But this is specifically not because of any resurgent loyalty. Rather, it is because "it was useless to think of such a possibility. His education had been that success for that mighty blue machine was certain; that it would make victories as a contrivance turns out buttons", which in itself is an interesting example of the victory of preconceived "truth" over manifest reality.

Neither does his triumphant conduct on the second day of the battle reflect a resurgent loyalty. Far from losing "concern for himself," or becoming "not a man but a member," his private urgencies constantly impelled him to set himself apart from the body of the regiment, both physically and mentally. Thus his "'wild cat'" conduct in the first action, his assertion of himself alongside Lieutenant Hasbrouck in front of the regiment's colors, and his seizing the flag. As their attack faltered and they began to retreat, he was mortified, enraged that his hope for "a fine revenge upon the officer who had referred to him and his fellows as mule drivers" could not "come to pass." It is not a baffled loyalty to the regiment that is uppermost in his mind. His "blackened face was held toward the enemy, but his greater hatred was riveted upon the man, who, not knowing him, had called him a mule driver". When he recognized the "bitter justice" in the taunts from the "veterans" that witnessed the regiment's failure, "He veiled a glance of disdain at his fellows". He was stung anew by the brigade commander's public criticism of the regiment; but when word came to Private Fleming that he and Private Wilson had been singled out for praise by Colonel MacChesnay, he "speedily forgot many things. The past held no pictures of error and disappointment".

Private Fleming's penultimate delight was entirely concentrated upon himself: upon his "deeds" and "performances," and the "respectful comments" he had won from his fellow soldiers. There is no suggestion he took any pride in the regiment's accomplishments or felt any particular loyalty toward its future—despite the public role he was going to play in that future as its color sergeant. When he did look "at his companions," he did so "stealthily," and with "suspicion" that they might see into his darker secrets: he was redeemed from his anxiety by the dull-witted mediocrity of the dialog surrounding him. His final satisfaction and contentment was completely personal, set explicitly against what had befallen the army: "The procession of weary soldiers became a be-draggled train, despondent and muttering, marching with churning effort in a trough of liquid brown mud under a low, wretched sky. Yet the youth smiled, for he saw that the world was a world for him, though many discovered it to be made of oaths and walking sticks". His personal contentment was at odds with, was in point of fact disloyal to, the army in this hour of its disheartening defeat, disloyal as well to the cause and country depending upon that army.

Qualities Absent from Fleming's Heroism

In thus refuting conventional (or what are often assumed to be conventional) attitudes concerning the valuable lessons in discipline and loyalty that are instilled by warfare and military service, *The Red Badge of Courage* is similar to a great body of specifically "antiwar" fictional narratives. Military discipline it-self becomes the enemy in such fictions as [E.E. Cummings's] *The Enormous Room* and such films as [Sidney Lumet's] "The Hill." Its brutalizing rather than redemptive quality is the sub-ject of [Stanley Kubrick's] "Full Metal Jacket." The full fury of [Erich Maria Remarque's] *All Quiet on the Western Front* is fo-cused upon the authority figures who instilled martial and pa-triotic loyalties in innocent schoolboys.

In Crane's novel, it is the way in which these attitudes are refuted that is atypical. Military discipline is not characterized by brutal monsters or by monstrous injustices. Discipline is simply nonexistent—and with interestingly various conse-quences. It is the same with loyalty to cause or country: rather than proving empty or obscenely misleading, to this novel's hero it is just nonexistent. Nonetheless in these two matters Crane's novel does not depart (so to speak, since again it actu-ally precedes the post–World War I tradition) in substance from the tradition of the antiwar fictional narrative.

A Parody of Romanticized War Literature

Amy Kaplan

Amy Kaplan is a professor of English at the University of Pennsylvania. She is the author of The Social Construction of American Realism *and* The Anarchy of Empire in the Making of U.S. Culture.

In the viewpoint that follows, Kaplan states that in the decades after the American Civil War, novelists began reenvisioning the conflict, portraying it not as a deep-seated political struggle with lingering tensions between North and South but as a framework for romantic escapades and narratives that saluted martial valor. Because it, too, set itself apart from larger questions about the divisions that plagued the nation in the war's aftermath, The Red Badge of Courage *was somewhat akin to other war-related novels of its day, Kaplan claims. In her view, however, Stephen Crane refused to accept the overly idealized literary conventions that made the Civil War seem a chivalrous affair. Though Crane allowed his main character to indulge in such fancies, Kaplan insists that Crane himself mocked these false ideals and depicted warfare as a gritty, unromantic, and ultimately disillusioning experience.*

The year that saw the publication of *The Red Badge of Courage* to great acclaim on both sides of the Atlantic was reviewed as a time of "wars and bloodshed" by Joseph Pulitzer's New York *World*. The newspaper's year-end survey of 1895 recalled that "from Japan westward to Jackson's Hole, bloodshed has encircled the globe," and it listed some examples of contemporary wars:

Amy Kaplan, from "The Spectacle of War in Crane's Revision of History," in *New Essays on "The Red Badge of Courage,"* edited by Lee Clark Mitchell, Cambridge University Press, 1986. Copyright © Cambridge University Press 1986. Reprinted with the permission of Cambridge University Press and the author.

When the year 1895 dawned the Italians were engaged in a bloody war with the Abyssinians; Haiti was overrun by rebels, who had burned the capital, Port-au-Prince, and slaughtered many people; the French were preparing for their disastrous if victorious war in Madagascar; the Dutch were slaughtering the natives of Lombok, one of their dependencies in southeastern Asia; and rebellions were in progress in several of the South American countries.

To newspaper readers in 1895, these outbreaks of international violence may have seemed remote from America's geographical borders and even more distant in time from the historic battlefields of America's last major conflict, the Civil War. Yet as the decade progressed, the United States ventured more boldly into international disputes; after verging on military engagements with Italy, Chile, and Britain in the early 1890's. America fought a war against Spain in Cuba and the Philippines in 1898. Mass-circulation newspapers like the *World*, which had already made exotic battles in European colonies a staple for American consumption, had an enthusiastic audience feasting on the spectacle of the Spanish-American War. One year after covering the Greco-Turkish War, Stephen Crane landed in Cuba with the American marines as a special correspondent for Pulitzer. Datelined June 22, 1898, the *World* headline for the first major battle of the Spanish-American War read: "THE RED BADGE OF COURAGE WAS HIS WIG-WAG [WARNING] FLAG."

Reimagining War

What do these international wars have to do with *The Red Badge of Courage*, a novel begun in 1893 about an internecine [within a group] conflict that took place thirty years earlier? Although Crane himself had not yet seen a battle when he wrote his book, the heightened militarism in America and Europe at the end of the nineteenth century shapes his novel as much as does the historical memory of the Civil War. Crane's novel participates in a widespread cultural movement to reinterpret the war as the birth of a united nation assuming global power and to revalue the legitimacy of military activity in general. The novel looks back at the Civil War to map a new arena into which modern forms of warfare can be imaginatively projected.

This conjunction of past and present may help explain the paradoxical status that *The Red Badge of Courage* has long held as *the* classic American Civil War novel that says very little about that war. Crane divorces the Civil War from its historical context by conspicuously avoiding the political, military, and geographical coordinates of the 1860s, and he equally divorces the conflict from a traditional literary context by rejecting generic narrative conventions. The novel reduces both history and the historical novel to what its main character thinks of as "crimson blotches on the page of the past." The illegibility of history in Crane's war novel has informed most critical approaches, which either treat it as a statement about war in general, turn war into a metaphor for psychological or metaphysical conflicts, reconstruct the absent historical referents of the Civil War battlefield, or decry the weakness of the historical imagination in American literature. Contrary to these critical assumptions, Crane wrenches the war from its earlier contexts, not to banish history from his "Episode" but to reinterpret the war through the cultural lenses and political concerns of the late nineteenth century.

If, on the battlefield of *The Red Badge of Courage*, Crane does not revisit old territory with a historical imagination, he does explore an unfamiliar social landscape reminiscent of the modern cityscape of his earlier writing and replete with similar social tensions. Like other well-known novels of its time, Crane's is a book about social change, about the transition not only from internecine to international conflict or from preindustrial to mechanized forms of warfare, but also from traditional to modern modes of representation. The novel implicitly contributes to and criticizes the contemporary militarization of American culture by focusing not on politics but on the problem of representing war. Crane transforms the representation of war from a shared experience that can be narrated in written or oral stories into an exotic spectacle that must be viewed by a spectator and conveyed to an audience. This transformation was to provide Crane with a lens for reporting the real wars he observed in Greece and Cuba only two years after writing his Civil War novel.

Creating a Soldier's War

To read *The Red Badge of Courage* historically, it is necessary to understand how Crane's contemporaries were reinterpreting the Civil War, for Crane was not alone in divorcing the conflict from its historical context and formulating a new one. In the outpour of nonfiction and fiction in the 1880s, writers consistently avoided referring to political conflicts over slavery or secession in favor of the theme of national reconciliation. In both genteel magazines and dime novels, the "road to reunion" look the form of glorifying the heroism and valor of the soldiers in both armies. Memoirs of the war depicted soldiers on both sides chatting and singing together on guard duty and cheering one another in the midst of battle as they rescued the wounded. Such memories led one author to conclude that "had the work of reconstruction been left to the fighting men of the North and South, much of the bitterness of that period would have been avoided." The bonds between soldiers in the field were seen to outlast and transcend the political conflicts for which they fought.

Crane's source for *The Red Badge of Courage*, the popular *Battles and Leaders of the Civil War*, epitomized this trend. To instruct a new generation in the meaning of the war in 1884, the editors of *The Century Magazine* invited veterans from both the Union and Confederate armies to record in detail their memories of major battles with the purpose of facilitating mutual respect, "the strongest bond of a united people." In their preface to the four-volume edition in 1887, the editors took partial credit for that fact that

> coincident with the progress of the series during the past three years may be noted a marked increase in the number of fraternal meetings between Union and Confederate veterans, enforcing the conviction that the nation is restored in spirit as in fact, and that each side is contributing its share to the new heritage of manhood and peace.

These memoirs and meetings radically reinterpreted the meaning of the battlefield itself. No longer an arena for enacting political conflict, it became a site for transcending conflict through the mutual admiration of military prowess.

Romance and Reconciliation

Fiction about the Civil War in the 1880s reinforced the theme of reconciliation by using romantic subplots to frame the battle scenes. In the traditional genre of the historical romance, heroism on the battlefield was rewarded by the love of the heroine at home; the plots often revolved around a love affair between a Union soldier and a Southern girl or around the division and reunion of kinsmen fighting on opposing sides. If memoirs hailed the reunion among men on the battlefield, fiction suggested that "neither the war nor reconstruction produced problems which could not be solved . . . by an adequately consummated marriage" [as critic Robert A. Lively writes]. During the postreconstruction period, both military histories and domestic fiction excised political conflict from the collective memory of the Civil War.

If the spirit of national unity could be abstracted from the devastating four-year conflict, the ideal of martial valor could be further abstracted from the goal of national unity. Participants and observers alike later viewed the battlefield of the Civil War as a testing ground for the virility and courage of the individual soldier, independent of any broader national aim. . . .

The Resurgence of Knights, Swashbucklers, and Barbarians

In fiction, the discovery of the primitive and the celebration of the martial ideal joined together in trends as diverse as naturalism and the historical romance. The adventure tales of Robert Louis Stevenson were more widely read in the United States than in England, and Kipling remained one of the most popular writers in both countries throughout the 1890s. Kipling's *The Light That Failed* (1891), with its double focus on the bohemian artist in Europe and the imperial battlefields of the Orient, exerted a strong influence on American naturalists such as Crane, [Frank] Norris, and [Jack] London. While they explored the atavistic [reversion to the past] qualities of modern life and often universalized war as a metaphor for the social Darwinian struggle, the historical romance, which appealed to a similar ethos, underwent a popular revival on both sides of the Atlantic. . . .

Romances about crusaders, questing knights, and fantastic kingdoms did not only look back nostalgically toward a lost wholeness; they also projected fanciful realms for contemporary adventures and the exercise of military power. William Dean Howells was not the only critic to relate the "swashbuckler swashing on his buckler" to the arousal of jingoism [extreme nationalism] and the clamor for foreign wars in the 1890s. The lament for the closing of the frontier was often coupled with a call for opening new frontiers abroad to release the pressure of class conflict brewing at home, and the discovery of the primitive—in the wilds and within—similarly coincided with the discovery of primitive people to control in exotic places. Chivalric nostalgia existed side by side with the rationalization and modernization of the armed forces; the critique of overcivilization bolstered the onward march of "civilization," and the discovery of barbaric impulses within modern man would be enacted on a battlefield of "uncivilized" frontiers, such as Cuba and the Philippines. . . .

Child soldiers huddle together in fear in this still from John Huston's film adaptation of The Red Badge of Courage. *Crane's novel exposed the grim realities of war at a time when war novels tended to romanticize conflict.* © Bettmann/Corbis.

Crane's Parody of Genre Conventions

In *The Red Badge of Courage*, Crane not only contributes to the contemporary abstraction of the Civil War from its historical context but also takes the further step of challenging those popular tales that recontextualize the war. As [Crane scholar] Eric Solomon has established, parody provides a central narrative strategy in all of Crane's writing. His war novel does more than parody either generic conventions or historical novels about the Civil War; it specifically parodies those narrative forms used to reinterpret the Civil War and to imagine new kinds of warfare in the 1890s.

The problem of reinterpreting the past to anticipate the immediate future is thematized in the first chapter of *The Red Badge of Courage*. Following the silent panorama of the battlefield in the opening paragraph, the novel bursts into a noisy state of anticipation: To plot in advance their upcoming initiation, recruits trade rumors about "brilliant campaigns" and veterans exchange tales of former battles to reimagine the enemy they will soon face. The central character, Henry Fleming, reexamines the stories he has heard about war in order to question what course his own actions might take. Throughout the first chapter, the narrator similarly evokes contemporary narratives of the Civil War and of the chivalric romance to test their applicability to his own story that lies ahead.

The second paragraph of the novel mocks the revival of the medieval romance by using chivalric rhetoric to describe the mundane activity of a soldier doing his laundry: "Once a certain tall soldier developed virtues and went resolutely to wash a shirt. He came flying back from a brook waving his garment, banner-like. He was swelled with a tale." The pose the soldier adopts of "herald in red and gold" is similarly deflated by his news, which sounds like small-town gossip, "heard from a reliable friend who had it from a truthful cavalryman who had heard it from his trustworthy brother." Both the medium and the message of these insubstantial rumors reveal the powerlessness of the recruits and the inadequacy of their tales to anticipate their fate.

The third paragraph of the novel suggests the social function of these chivalric stories for readers at the end of the century. The rumors of "a brilliant campaign" draw an audience of soldiers away from "a negro teamster who had been dancing upon a cracker-box." In the 1880s, tales of chivalric exploits similarly superseded the older narrative of emancipation at a time when reconciliation was effected at the cost of undoing the gains of former slaves after the war. In this only reference to blacks in the novel, Crane both divorces his own "episode" from any former stories about freeing the slaves and calls attention to the process whereby the history of emancipation had been reduced to a form of entertainment. The "deserted" teamster sits "mournfully down" to lament his loss of an audience and his own passing as a figure for the subject of emancipation from the narrative landscape of the Civil War battlefield.

Deflating the Martial Ethos

In the first chapter, Crane similarly evokes and discards the domestic subplot, which provided an important structure in both Civil War romances and regional fiction. Thwarting Henry's expectation of a noble farewell, his mother deflates his romantic aspirations and reminds him that he is "jest one little feller 'mongst a hull lot'a others." When the regiment leaves his village, Henry catches a glimpse of a "dark girl," whom he thinks grows "sad and demure at the sight of his blue and brass." Like the "negro teamster," the "dark girl" mourns her own passing from the novel as a figure of the domestic subplot. Throughout the novel, domestic images resurface only to deflate the martial ethos rather than to validate it, as troops are compared to women trying on bonnets or to brooms sweeping up the battlefield.

In addition to rejecting these narratives of emancipation and domesticity, Crane parodies the memoirs of veterans that were so popular in the 1880s. The first chapter presents a commonplace scene in which Henry recalls chatting with a Confederate sentinel:

> "Yank", the other had informed him, "yer a right dum good feller.' This sentiment, floating to him upon the still air, had made him temporarily regret war."

Here the familiar encomium [warm praise] for the valor of the enemy is reduced to barely articulate mutual recognition. Crane follows this set piece with the recruit's distrust of veterans:

> Various veterans had told him tales. Some talked of grey, bewhiskered hordes who were advancing, with relentless curses and chewing tobacco with unspeakable valor; tremendous

bodies of fierce soldiery who were sweeping along like the Huns. Others spoke of tattered eternally-hungry men who fired despondent powder.

The veterans' accounts of the past prove no more reliable than the rumors that the recruits project about the future. These stories create a mythical alien enemy that no more prepares Henry for battle than the mirror image of the foe as a "dum good feller." Indeed, Henry finds that "he could not put a whole faith in veterans' tales, for recruits were their prey".

Crane's parody questions the pedagogical value of those memoirs that made up such popular works as *Battle and Leaders*. In a well-known letter, Crane dismissed these volumes for their content, for their lack of information about the subjective response to the battlefield—"they won't tell me what I want to know." In the opening of his novel, he rejects them as a form, as a narrative mode inadequate not only for historical accuracy but also for the representation of warfare in the 1890s. More broadly, Crane undermines both the authority of veterans to transmit their knowledge to a younger generation of soldiers and the power of historical memory to assure continuity into the present.

Fleming Clings to the Chivalric Ideal

Although the novel opens by dismissing equally the narrative of emancipation, the domestic subplot of fiction, and the memoirs of veterans, the chivalric narrative outlasts the others as the main character clings to it tenaciously. . . . Henry Fleming's inner aspirations are composed of ideas in the popular books he reads and clichés that circulate around him. Henry imagines himself most often as a medieval knight, who in his late-nineteenth-century manifestation combines violent adventure with primitive virility. If Henry's dreams are rendered as lurid chivalric exploits, his rational skepticism is also cast in the rhetoric of strenuosity. When Henry first considers enlisting, for example, he imagines battles to be "things of the bygone with his thought-images of heavy crowns and high castles". In Henry's suspicion of the present war, the narrator mocks the "warrior critique" of an overcivilized society by twice repeating the refrainlike formula: "Greeklike struggles would be no more. Men were better, or more timid. Secular and religious education had effaced the throat-grappling instinct or else firm finance held in check the passions." Like many of Crane's contemporaries, however, Henry hopes that the battle will prove him wrong and will thrust him beyond the mundane commercial world into a realm of primitive abandon.

Despite the narrative parody, Henry does find these hopes fulfilled on the battlefield, where he resurrects the image of the medieval warrior. As he anticipates the battle, for example, he imagines himself as a dragon fighter, and he later flees from "an onslaught of redoubtable dragons." When he does fight, after returning to the regiment, he sees himself as a medieval warrior who has finally penetrated the primitive depths:

> It was revealed to him that he had been a barbarian, a beast. He had fought like a pagan who defends his religion. Regarding it, he saw that it was fine, wild and, in some ways, easy. He had been a tremendous figure, no doubt. By this struggle, he had overcome obstacles which he had admitted to be mountains. They had fallen like paper peaks and he was now what he called a hero. And he had not been aware of the process. He had slept and, awakening, found himself a knight.

After the next fight, he feels that he has reached a frontier and entered "some new and unknown land". Crane represents Henry's battle experience as the return to a premodern era, as the exploration of an uncivilized frontier, and as the recovery of a primitive self in a dreamlike preconscious state. Crane's language becomes enmeshed in the rhetoric of strenuosity that it parodies as his narrative discovers the primitive and revives the martial ideal on the Civil War battlefield of the 1890s.

Military Discipline in
The Red Badge of Courage

Robert M. Myers

Robert M. Myers is an associate professor of English and the chair of the English Department at Lock Haven University in Pennsylvania. He has published scholarly articles in American Literary Realism, Stephen Crane Studies, *and* War, Literature & the Arts.

In the following viewpoint, Myers maintains that although Civil War officers could and did inspire their troops to stand firm in combat, typical soldiers at the time relied on internal discipline to remain effective on the battlefield. According to Myers, in The Red Badge of Courage, *Henry Fleming's military training is overwhelmed early on by his instinct to survive, and he flees from a firefight. And while Fleming wanders for some time with his thought of shame and cowardice, he learns to use these self-policing mechanisms to prove himself a man in his next engagement. As Myers notes, Fleming eventually stands firm and even charges into battle, earning the praise of his officers. By the end of the novel, Fleming has gained new courage, in Myers's opinion, and even conforms to military rule when he realizes that acceptance and recognition from his peers and his superiors results from his prowess in battle.*

After the battle of First Bull Run [in July 1861], [Union] General William Tecumseh Sherman complained, "I doubt if our democratic form of government admits of that organization and discipline without which an army is a mob." Throughout the war, military discipline would remain prob-

Robert M. Myers, "The Subtle Battle Brotherhood: The Construction of Military Discipline in *The Red Badge of Courage*," *War, Literature, and the Arts: An International Journal of the Humanities*, 1999, pp. 128–140. Copyright © 1999 by Robert M. Myers. Reproduced by permission of the author.

lematic for both armies. Union Colonel Thomas Wentworth Higginson argued that officers faced a challenge in disciplining an army composed of individuals raised in a democratic tradition:

> Three years are not long enough to overcome the settled habits of twenty years. The weak point of our volunteer service invariably lies here, that the soldier, in nine cases out of ten, utterly detests being commanded, while the officer, in his turn, equally shrinks from commanding. . . .

Internal and External Authority

One possible response was to emphasize the supervisory role of the officer. Writing in 1864, Higginson insisted that the war had conclusively demonstrated the need for a well-trained corps of officers. Noting some of the derelictions that he had personally witnessed—neglect of picket duty and failure to maintain sanitary conditions—Higginson argued that the blame must always fall on the officers:

> The officer makes the command, as surely, as, in educational matters, the teacher makes the school. There is not a regiment in the army so good that it could not be utterly spoiled in three months by a poor commander, nor so poor that it could not be altogether transformed in six by a good one. The difference in material is nothing,—white or black, German or Irish; so potent is military machinery that an officer who knows his business can make good soldiers out of almost anything, give him but a fair chance.

For Higginson the power of this potent military machinery depended on the correct placement of the "raw material" in a system of observation and hierarchy. He insisted, "The newest recruit soon grows steady with a steady corporal at his elbow, a well-trained sergeant behind him, and a captain or a colonel whose voice means something to give commands".

However, Higginson's belief in the efficacy of the officer, a visibly placed external authority, was not the only model of military discipline in circulation by the turn of the century. Ellwood Bergey's 1903 book, *Why Soldiers Desert from the United States Army*, attacks the system of military discipline as a threat to the American belief in the dignity of the individual:

> On entering the army the young man must sacrifice every atom of manhood and dignity in order to comply with the foppish rules of the Army Regulations, which are enforced with demon-like persistence. He must bow in servile obedience to the most accomplished bacchanalian that holds an army commission. No vas[s]al or slave was ever required to show greater humility to their masters than the soldiers of the United States Army are required to show toward their "superior" officers.

Bergey is careful to point out that eliminating this "servile obedience" would not undermine true military discipline. Using "our great industrial establishments" as an example, Bergey suggests that the most efficient workers or soldiers are the product of internal rather than external discipline. . . .

The tension between external and internal models of military discipline is represented in *The Red Badge of Courage*. As Henry Fleming is transformed from a raw recruit to an effective soldier, his own vigilant internal gaze eliminates the need for constant supervision by his officers. Henry's disciplining reflects a broader tension in nineteenth-century American culture between a discourse that celebrated the freedom of the autonomous individual and a discourse that emphasized the need for effective mechanisms of social control.

Fleming's Place in the Battlefield Hierarchy

Before he leaves for the war Henry's mother gives him advice that will become the foundation of his immersion in military discipline. To avoid doing anything shameful, he must always imagine that his actions are observed: "I don't want yeh to ever do anything, Henry, that yeh would be 'shamed to let me know about. Jest think as if I was a-watchin' yeh. If yeh keep that in yer mind allus, I guess yeh'll come out about right." She also encourages him to accept his place in military authority: "Yer jest one little feller amongst a hull lot of others and yeh've got to keep quiet an' do what they tell yeh". This advice is especially important given Henry's romantic dreams of "Greeklike" struggles where he imagines "peoples secure in the shadow of his eagle-eyed prowess". By the time of the Civil War, such individualistic heroics were anachronistic, if not actually counterproductive. Modern warfare required disciplined soldiers who recognized their place in the military hierarchy.

Henry's initial experiences in the army prepare him for this concept of warfare through strict regimentation: he is "drilled and drilled and reviewed, and drilled and drilled and reviewed". The repetitious drill is designed to establish the instinct of obedience to the officers, and the constant review begins the process of evaluation that will properly place the men within the military hierarchy. In camp Henry begins to internalize the army's code as he becomes his own observer and evaluator. He realizes that he is an "unknown quantity," and understands that "the only way to prove himself was to go into the blaze" and then "figuratively to watch his legs to discover their merits and faults". As he impatiently waits for this test, he becomes frustrated over the delays, and, curiously, the text seems to link his subversive complaints with veteran status: "Sometimes his anger at the commanders reached an acute stage, and he grumbled about the camp *like a veteran*" (my emphasis). This simile suggests that to fully develop the code of courage the soldier must have an element of insubordination.

As he approaches his first battle, the physical presence of the regiment provides a structure that contains Henry's fear: "He instantly saw that it would be impossible for him to escape from the regiment. It inclosed him. And there were iron laws of tradition and law on four sides. He was in a moving box". The representatives of military authority are visibly present: the company captain coaxes the men "in schoolmistress fashion", and the lieutenant beats Henry with his sword when he seems to be "skulking". During the actual fighting, Henry is reassured by the presence of his comrades about him: "He felt the subtle battle brotherhood more potent even than the cause for which they were fighting". But the limitations of external mechanisms of discipline are exposed in the second engagement. When Henry mistakenly believes that his regiment is fleeing, he is left to his own, yet undeveloped, resources, and his survival instincts overwhelm his military training. The external control of the military authority, in this case, the lieutenant, is unable to stop his flight:

> The lieutenant sprang forward bawling. The youth saw his features wrathfully red, and saw him make a dab with his sword. His one thought of the incident was that the lieutenant was a peculiar creature to feel interested in such matters upon this occasion.

Fleming's Desertion

Henry's desertion is an extreme breach of military discipline, yet his thoughts reveal that his flight never removes him from the terms of military authority. Henry's initial rationalizations attempt to rewrite his cowardice as sound military strategy:

> He had done a good part in saving himself, who was a little piece of the army. He had considered the time, he said, to be one in which it was the duty of every little piece to rescue itself if possible. Later the officers could fit the little pieces together again, and make a battle-front. If none of the little pieces were wise enough to save themselves from the flurry of death at such a time, why, then, where would be the army? It was all plain that he had proceeded according to very correct and commendable rules.

Of course, this subversion of military discipline, which demands obedience of privates rather than discretion, is subverted by Crane's irony. As readers, we know that no such thoughts were in Henry's mind at the moment of his flight, and the absurdity of his strategy has been made apparent by the general, who is delighted that Henry's regiment has held its position. Likewise, Henry's later attempts to justify his behavior are undercut by his encounters with the dead man, the tattered man, and Jim Conklin. When Henry sees their bodies, visibly marked with the evidence of their obedience, he realizes the extent of his own violation of the code of courage. Lacking a wound, he believes that his cowardice is visible: "He now felt that his shame could be viewed. He was continually casting sidelong glances to see if the men were contemplating the letters of guilt he felt burned into his brow". To Henry the tattered man's innocent questions assert "a society that probes pitilessly at secrets until all is apparent". Henry's fear of detection leads him to worry that in future engagements his regiment "would try to keep watch of him to discover when he would run", and he imagines himself subject to their collective gaze: "Then, as if the heads were moved by one muscle, all the faces were turned toward him with wide, derisive, grins. . . . He was a slang phrase". Henry's shame is not actually visible but the persistent ocular imagery makes it clear that his violation of the code of courage has made him into his own observer. His desire for escape from this imagined gaze leads him to wish for a visible mark of heroism, "a wound, a red badge of courage". When he is wounded by a retreating soldier from his own army, his confidence is restored because he can now evade the gaze of the army: "He did not shrink from an encounter with the eyes of judges, and allowed no thoughts of his own to keep him from an attitude of manfulness. He had performed his mistakes in the dark, so he was still a man". But Henry's thoughts make it clear that the inefficient surveillance of the army has been replaced by his own internal gaze, as his awareness of his transgression inscribes the code of courage. Henry realizes that he is still "below the standard of traditional man-hood" and feels "abashed when confronting memories of some men he had seen."

Becoming a Self-Disciplined Soldier

Henry's three engagements on the second day complete his movement from external to internal discipline. In the first battle, his animal instincts take over and he fights viciously, even after the enemy has retreated. While he is in front of the line, fighting alone, Henry's comrades "seemed all to be engaged in staring with astonishment at him. They had become spectators". Having acted heroically in the eyes of the army, Henry can now view himself as a hero:

> Regarding it, he saw that it was fine, wild, and, in some ways, easy. He had been a tremendous figure, no doubt. By this struggle he had overcome obstacles which he had admitted to be mountains. They had fallen like paper peaks, and he was now what he called a hero.

Even though Henry has acted in an undisciplined manner—he has pressed forward in advance of his regiment and has continued to discharge his rifle even though the enemy is no longer present—the lieutenant, a shrewd officer, reinforces Henry's newly constructed self by praising him. But to be a good soldier, Henry must still integrate courage and discipline. Ironically, all that is necessary to complete Henry's disciplining is a sense of resentment against his officers.

Before the next engagement Henry overhears the general dismiss his regiment as "mule drivers" who could easily be sacrificed. His anger at the general surfaces when the lieutenant encourages Henry to continue the stalled attack, even grappling "with him as if for a wrestling bout". In frustration, and feeling "a sudden unspeakable indignation against his officer," Henry defiantly leads the charge, even picking up the flag when the color bearer is shot. When the attack fails, Henry is frustrated because he had hoped that his actions would force the general to re-evaluate his regiment's worth: "He had pictured red letters of curious revenge. 'We *are* mule drivers, are we?' And now he was compelled to throw them away". Likewise, in the final engagement, Henry is willing to stand firm, even to his death, which would be "a poignant retaliation" upon the general:

> In all the wild graspings of his mind for a unit responsible for his sufferings and commotions he always seized upon the man who had dubbed him wrongly. And it was his idea, vaguely formulated, that his corpse would be *for those eyes* a great and salt reproach. (my emphasis)

The extent to which Henry's anger leads to his total immersion in military discipline is suggested by the "tranquil philosophy" he expresses after the regiment overhears the general's contemptuous dismissal. Henry reassures Wilson that the general "probably didn't see nothing of it at all and got mad as blazes, and concluded we were a lot of sheep, just because we didn't do what he wanted done". He wishes that Grandpa Henderson had been there to witness it for "he'd have known that we did our best and fought good", and he basks in the praise of the colonel and lieutenant, who label him "a jimhickey," and suggest that he should be a major-general. No longer concerned with larger questions of strategy, which are properly the domain of the generals, Henry submits himself to the expectations of his immediate officers. Thus, cowardly desertion produces heroism, and resentment against the officers produces passive acceptance of military hierarchy.

The Army in the New Industrial Age

Daniel Shanahan

Daniel Shanahan is a professor of communications in the Humanities Faculty of Charles University in Prague, Czech Republic. He is the author of Towards a Genealogy of Individualism *and* Language, Feeling and the Brain: The Evocative Vector.

As the United States experienced a growth in industrialization in the early nineteenth century, American writers confronted the changes that the burgeoning capitalist system was wreaking on the nation. In Maggie: A Girl of the Streets, *Stephen Crane wrote of slum life and the Darwinian competitiveness that pushed some people up the social ladder while keeping others down. In the following viewpoint, Shanahan expands on this theme. He claims that in* The Red Badge of Courage, *Crane portrayed the military as a machine that suppressed the individuality of soldiers to foreground regimen and purpose. At the same time, Crane insists that competition among soldiers to prove their bravery helped the machine function as an effective fighting force. According to Shanahan, both the industrial age metaphors of competitiveness and mechanization reveal Crane's awareness of the social transformation in his times. In Shanahan's estimation, however, Crane also uses irony to expose the change to his readers and carve out some artistic distance for himself.*

In 1904, four years after the death of his friend Stephen Crane, [American novelist and social critic] Henry James returned to the United States for the first time in twenty-one years. He describes his approach to New York City this way:

Daniel Shanahan, "The Army Motif in *The Red Badge of Courage* as a Response to Industrial Capitalism," *Papers on Language and Literature*, vol. 32, no. 4, Fall 1996. Copyright © 1996 by The Board of Trustees, Southern Illinois University at Edwardsville. Reproduced by permission.

... the monster grows and grows ... becoming ... some co-
lossal set of clockworks, some steel-souled machine room of
brandished arms and hammering fists and opening and
closing jaws. The immeasurable bridges are but as the hori-
zontal sheaths of pistons working at high pressure, day and
night ...

This was the New York which, in the two short decades of
James's absence, had replaced the prosaic city of James's youth;
this new city of motion and machines was the New York Crane
had lived in as he wrote *The Red Badge of Courage*. It was a
city that, like the country it represented, had been [according
to historian Jay Martin] "seized by change".

Indeed, probably nothing could better characterize the period of James's absence than the overwhelming transformation and retransformation that America underwent from 1880
to 1900. And the forces behind the changes which took place
in those years were largely those which underlie James's description of New York: the impetus of capitalism and industrialization, of the competitive drive to succeed and the machine
which helped make success possible. As [scholar] Larzer Ziff
points out, the early literary response to the social upheaval
created in America by capitalism and industrialization was
ambiguous—and weak. The problem was not lack of talent: it
was lack of vision. As Ziff suggests of the architectural establishment of the time, writers who had grown up in pre–Civil
War America "yearned to impose upon the whirl of late-
nineteenth-century America the dream of stasis, an ideal and
all-covering beauty ... Static idealization of the human condition seemed to be the answer to the impossibly unaesthetic
whirl of social conditions". But what was needed was a vision
which would unify the "unaesthetic whirl" without confining
it, and to achieve that vision a writer would have to be willing
to allow the whirl to emerge without bending it to his own
purposes. Didacticism, ideal or apocalyptic, could easily betray
the integrity of any attempt to distill the temper of the times
into a literary work....

Competition and Contention in the Army

Crane wrote *The Red Badge of Courage* immediately after *Maggie: A Girl of the Streets*, a novel which presents a vision of contemporary society as a ruthlessly competitive domain in which all men—and women—are reduced to their predatory instincts and all of their distinguishing characteristics are effaced by the brutality to which they themselves become subject. The effects of emergent capitalism on American society are never far from view in *Maggie*, and given the novel's highly competitive social environment, it comes as no surprise that the theme of competition so thoroughly informs *Red Badge*. From the opening moments of the book, in which Crane portrays two soldiers arguing over rumors about troop movements, to the near-brawl that erupts before the first chapter closes—this time about how well the regiment will fight—contention is the dominant mode of social interaction. In the world Crane creates, the army is rife with internal contention even before it enters into the grand competition by which, [socialist theorist Karl] Marx had argued only a few years before, industrial capitalism sustains itself.

But throughout the first half of the novel, the main character, Henry Fleming, is an exception to the rule of contention and competition as the dominant mode of behavior, and while it is common to see Henry as a character taken from romantic idealism about war to a tempered bravery, it is less common to see how Henry's reluctance to compete, and his later willingness to do so, punctuate his change in character.

Because he seems to lack the innate competitive instincts of the other men in the regiment, Henry never takes part in any of the arguing, sparring or contending that goes on between his fellows. In short, he fails to communicate with them on the terms in which they most frequently seem to communicate with one another, so he remains an outsider, and only nominally a member of the army. Only after he witnesses the death of his friend, Jim Conklin, does Henry begin to show signs of adopting the aggressiveness he will need to face the realities of war. Moments after Jim's violent death, Henry makes "a furious motion" in response to the tattered soldier's questions about Henry's non-existent wound; Henry became "as one at bay" and he feels "the quiver of war desire." This is the first competitive flicker in Henry's character, and its appearance marks his readiness for the "red badge" which will initiate him into the fellowship of his social environment.

Fleming's Growing Competitive Zeal

Surprisingly little has been made of the fact that Henry's "wound," the red badge of "courage" which marks the turning point in his character development, comes neither from the enemy nor even from a random unidentifiable bullet: it comes from one of his own men, a soldier fleeing wildly, as Henry did, and who perceives Henry as merely another opposing force, another competitor. In this pivotal moment, Henry is attempting to communicate; however, he cannot see that his attempt has only one meaning in the lexicon of men each battling for his own survival: he is a threat to the soldier. And as a consequence, Henry receives the one response which makes sense: the man floors him with a single, vicious blow from his rifle—used, by a man in his most primitively competitive frame of mind, as a club.

Ironically, but not surprisingly, given that from the outset of the novel contention has been the currency of social communication, it is this blow from a comrade that punctuates the end of Henry's isolation from his fellows and initiates him into their ranks. Henceforth he is truly a member of the army, and as time goes on he reveals the effect of that initiation by becoming supremely competitive. Markedly contentious on several occasions during the night and morning after his return to the regiment, Henry enters battle with "his teeth set in a curlike snarl"; "he lost everything but his hate, his desire to smash into pulp the glittering smile of victory which he could feel upon the faces of his enemies." Not surprisingly, Henry shines in battle, possessed by "the spirit of a savage religion-mad," engulfed in "wild battle madness," and awaiting "the crushing blow that would prostrate the resistance."

In short, by the end of the novel Henry has reached the apotheosis of competition: he has become a true predator, and as such he demonstrates William Graham Sumner's belief "that the struggle for existence and the competition of life . . . draw out the highest achievements". Congratulated by his fellows for his performance and complimented by his superiors, Henry ultimately finds himself a deeply different person for his experience. "He was," Crane tells us, "a man" and, of course, he has also become "one of the men" in a way he could not previously. He has joined the army—that motif which seemed to carry such potency for writers trying to deal with the "unaesthetic whirl" of the late 19th century—he has found membership in society, and the catalyst of that discovery has been his acquiescence to the competitive spirit shared by his fellows. . . .

The Army as Machine

Crane uses mechanical imagery to position his novel on the pivot of the change wrought by the technological transformation of America wrought by industrialization, but because he does so without any overt didactic purposes, he comes much closer to making of the "unaesthetic whirl" what [Russian novelist Leo] Tolstoy had made of national pride in *War and Peace* and what [Czech author Franz] Kafka would make of faceless bureaucracy in *The Trial*: a vibrant undercurrent which transforms social realities into a lasting vision of the human condition.

Early on, in the first battle scene, machine imagery begins to appear after Henry has fired his first wild shot: "Directly," Crane says, "he was working at his weapon like an automatic

Civil war battle scene from John Huston's film adaptation of The Red Badge of Courage. *Crane's novel depicts an Industrial Age army that suppresses human individuality and functions as a machine.* Hulton Archive/Getty Images.

affair"; soon the entire regiment "wheezed and banged with a mighty power". Before long both Henry and the regiment are described in assembly-line images: clanking and clanging become the dominant sounds of the battle. This imagery pervades the novel. In the battle in which Henry flees, he imagines that the enemy "must be machines of steel"; the men who fail to run Henry calls "methodical idiots! Machine-like fools!". As he wanders aimlessly, Henry finds the battle "like the grinding of an immense and terrible machine", the purpose of which is to "produce corpses," and when he joins the wounded column he reflects how the "torn bodies expressed the awful machinery in which the men had been entangled". Even the death of his friend, Jim Conklin, takes on a machine-like quality: as it goes into its final death spasms, Conklin's body is like some engine wheezing and sputtering jerkily to a final halt, its broken gears causing the grotesque and halting dance of death. Indeed, in a later battle in which the regiment seems near its own death, Crane calls it "a machine run down".

Cogs in Motion

Machine imagery does not, however, account for the powerful evocation of turmoil Crane achieves. As [Crane biographer] R. W. Stallman long ago pointed out, "motion and change [are] . . . the dominant leitmotif of the book and a miniature form of its structure". Henry's initiation into the regiment's competitive, contentious mode of life is the consequence of having plunged himself into the motion of the battle; joining in the surging "blue demonstration," he becomes part of it and thereby achieves cog-like membership in his social environment. Similarly, when the flux of battle begins to dominate the novel, the battlefield itself takes on the appearance of a giant engine in which the armies are like pistons crashing to and fro in a wild orgy of mechanical power.

For example, late in the novel, as Henry and his comrades watch the battle from a distance, Crane describes the sound of the artillery as "the whirring and thumping of giant machinery"; then

> On an incline over which a road wound he saw wild and
> desperate rushes of men perpetually backward and forward
> in riotous surges. These parts of the opposing armies pitched
> upon each other madly at dictated points. To and fro they
> swelled.

While overtly the natural image of the sea, the to and fro motion, coupled with the "whirring and thumping of machinery" and the pitching of armies upon each other at "dictated points" make this passage strongly suggestive of piston motion. Unlike Henry Adams [the Bostonian author whose autobiography dealt mostly with his coming to grips with the advent of the twentieth century], who finds the steam engine and its mechanics too spiritless when compared to the dynamo, Crane finds in them the essence of the world of his time, plunging his readers headlong into the piston-like fury of the mechanical age—as his friend Henry James would when he returned to America four years after Crane's death.

This riot of motion continues as Henry and his regiment enter the final engagement of the battle. Twice Crane describes them as moving "to and fro", they begin to fire automatically, "without waiting for word of command." And as they approach the climactic confrontation with the enemy, Henry anticipates the moment this way:

> As he ran a thought of the shock of contact gleamed in his mind. He expected a great concussion when two bodies of troops crashed together. This became a part of his wild battle madness. He could feel the onwards swing of the regiment about him an he conceived of a thunderous, crushing blow that would prostrate the resistance and spread consternation and amazement for miles. The flying regiment was going to have a catapultian effect.

Here Crane reaches his crescendo: Henry has immersed himself in the regiment, the regiment plunges itself piston-like into the fray, and as they become caught up in the furious motion of battle, both Henry and his regiment, as we have seen, take on the attributes of predatory animals as Crane brings together the two churning forces which have created his world's "unaesthetic whirl": competition and technological change.

Fleming Becomes a Man of His Time

The question of whether Crane's vision of Henry is ironic has elicited a great deal of discussion among readers of the novel. But perhaps a passage Crane deleted from the final paragraphs of the novel's final version holds the key to understanding both Crane's attitude towards Henry and the world he creates for him and his comrades to inhabit. In the deleted passage. Crane says of Henry:

He was emerged from his struggles, with a large sympathy for the machinery of the universe. It was a deity laying about him with the bludgeon of correction ... He would no more stand upon places high and false, and denounce the distant planets. He beheld that he was tiny but not inconsequent to the sun. In the space-wide whirl of events no grain like him would be lost.

To look for Crane to approve or disapprove of Henry, or of the society of which he becomes a part, would be to attribute to Crane a didactic purpose which he did not have. His aim was to distill the essence of his time, not to show its potential ... or warn of its horror.... As an artist, Crane set out to capture the "unaesthetic whirl" in an aesthetic rendering that would preserve the dark tension of its beauty, and *Red Badge* is entirely consistent with that aim.

Unquestionably, Henry has changed by the novel's end; unquestionably, he has become more courageous and more selfless. He has even become more humble. But he has done so within a context that deals bludgeoning blows to its creatures. He has reacted involuntarily to those blows where one might prefer measured response; he has even learned to deal them himself, where one might hope he would refuse to do so; and he has given up the one thing which might have allowed him responsible refusal: his individuality. Yet at the same time he has matured over the course of the novel, he has become broader and more tested than he was at the novel's outset, and he no longer lives life as an alienated onlooker: he has jumped with both feet into his social context. In other words, by the end of the novel not only has Henry become, as Crane tells us, "a man", he has become a man of his time.

In that sense, Crane is much closer to Kafka than to Tolstoy. Just an Kafka takes one aspect of his own experience of contemporary life and uses the underlying purposelessness he finds there to portray the larger vacuity to which we may all be susceptible, Crane takes one aspect of his contemporary experience and uses it to develop a broader picture of the human condition. Crane uses the army and the war to portray the mass mentality which has begun to replace individualism in his time, to evoke the spirit of predatory competition which has begun to dominate the American landscape, and, at the same time, it affords him the opportunity to expose the powerful engines of change and motion which underlie this new, predatory mass society. And by avoiding ... didacticism ..., Crane creates for his readers a novel which is both of its time and at a distance from it, a vision which confronts the "unaesthetic whirl" and makes of it a truthful symmetry.

The Absurdity of Henry Fleming's Courage

Weihong Julia Zhu

An instructor at Central China Normal University, Weihong Julia Zhu has taught at Brigham Young University, Hawaii Campus, as part of an exchange program. She has published articles on Nathaniel Hawthorne and D.H. Lawrence as well as on Stephen Crane.

In the following viewpoint, Zhu argues that while Henry Fleming may have acted bravely in the latter part of The Red Badge of Courage, Stephen Crane undercuts any notion that his character's conduct is motivated by self-willed courage. Fleming is filled with romanticized notions of chivalrous combat, Zhu states, but the reality he faces is grim and void of any righteousness. In Zhu's view, Fleming tries to assert some pride by eventually standing firm in battle, yet even that is undermined by the falseness of his "badge of courage" and the lack of any moral cause that would make him understand the grander purpose of his fight. Crane furthermore diminishes Fleming's actions—and the actions of all the soldiers in the battle—by continually juxtaposing the insignificance of the armies with the grandeur of nature and its indifference to their petty conflict, Zhu asserts.

If the first controversy over *The Red Badge of Courage* centering on whether this novel was a work of art is a bygone one, the second one, which facilitates varied interpretations and explications, has never really been resolved. Among various issues, critics tend to argue over whether Henry Fleming is a hero or a coward. There is nothing wrong with such efforts. However, this tendency should in no case occur at the

Weihong Julia Zhu, "The Absurdity of Henry's Courage," *Stephen Crane Studies*, vol. 10, no. 2, Fall 2001, pp. 2–11. Copyright © 2001 *Stephen Crane Studies*. Reproduced by permission.

expense of something more important. Considering the thematic word in the title of this novel, readers may feel obliged to devote their attention to the topic of "courage" itself. In other words, this novel is not so much about whether Henry is a hero, as whether he exhibits reasonable courage at all. In the past some critics have observed the novel from this perspective. They contend that Crane's departure from the traditional ideas of heroism has made *The Red Badge of Courage* a worthy novel. Instead of promoting heroism, Crane demonstrates the absurdity of Henry's courage throughout the novel.

Illusion vs. Reality

Crane first reveals the absurdity of Henry's courage through a contrast between his illusion of heroic wars and the reality that betrays no trace of heroism. Journalistic duplicity encourages Henry to join the war. At first, he cannot make up his mind to enlist, but his heart "burn[s]" when he hears "tales of great movements" and reads of "marches, sieges, conflicts" and victories in the newspapers every day. He envisions all the heroic deeds and glory associated with war. However, his mother almost immediately disillusions him. When Henry tells his mother about his enlistment, he expects in excitement to see his mother's tears for him and prepares to return her sentiment with certain touching words. However, his mother neither cries nor utters any words that can facilitate his performance. Instead, her unexpected "contempt upon the quality of his war ardor and patriotism" irritates Henry.

If his mother's unanticipated response has not yet shattered his illusions, his inability to adapt to the disparity between illusion and reality dooms him to complete disillusionment in the battlefield. Henry has always dreamed of battles, viewing them as a series of "large pictures extravagant in color, lurid with breathless deeds". Unfortunately, what he witnesses after he joins the army runs counter to his dreams. First, he encounters apparently endless and monotonous waiting. For months Henry finds his fellow soldiers and himself either only on meaningless moves or in camps. Therefore, somewhat disappointed, he decides that "Greeklike struggles would be no more" because "men were better, or more timid". Then, when his regiment finally is to confront the enemy, one of the soldiers has to leave before any fight occurs. On the way to the battlefield, he trips and falls, having his three fingers crushed badly. This dramatic incident, according to [critic] John J. McDermott, relentlessly "challenges" Henry's "simple-minded" theory of courage. When he remembers his visions of "broken-bladed glory," he believes that they are "impossible pictures". His sudden and intense exposure to blood, bodies, horror, madness and chaos is the last straw. The battlefield scene differs so sharply from what he imagined that he is simply unable to react properly. Consequently, as [critic] Kevin J. Hayes insists, "since he cannot accommodate the discrepancy, he has no option but to run from battle". In justifying the cowardliness of Henry's flight, McDermott also puts blame on his deficient and "embryonic" understanding of courage. [Scholar] Chester L. Wolford supports these critics, noting that Crane has derided the conventional notions of heroism, and concluding that "*The Red Badge of Courage* is a denial of the epic view of history, which Crane felt creates an absurd, illusory, and vacuous emotion".

Examining Fleming's Motivation

The second way Crane chooses to exhibit the absurdity of Henry's courage is by revealing that courage as a motivation for Henry is distorted. According to [critic] Donald B. Gibson, the driving force of true heroism comes from the inside, from the power of one's mind. Conversely, Henry's courage derives from vanity. He is, as [critic] Howard C. Horsford remarks, obsessed with "self-image, to himself and in the eyes of others". When Henry first suspects himself to be capable of running away from the battle, he feels panicked and dismayed because he fears that the other new soldiers may possess greater confidence than he thinks he has. He continually constructs questions in order to probe this topic. Relieved when he receives an answer with a note of diffidence, he then feels like "a mental outcast" when he fails to detect any feelings akin to his own insecurity.

Ironically, others may not always see a person clearly. Crane, in the particular case of Henry, plants this irony in the "red badge of courage". Nobody suspects Henry's wound in the head to have resulted from an attack by a retreating soldier. The other soldiers show due respect for his wound and regard it as demonstration of Henry's courage. However, for Henry, who has envied the wounds of other soldiers and wished to have one himself, his "red badge of courage" feels burned and sore. Conscious of its origin, he has to fight fiercely to cover up his initial cowardice. He pushes his friend Wilson away and succeeds in obtaining the right to carry the unit flag. Unfortunately, even this epic action does not escape Crane's irony. Crane shows readers that Henry would rather his friend had possessed the flag, had he not felt the necessity of declaring his offer. Therefore, Horsford says, since this apparent heroism is not "conscious, willed intention," it weighs no more heavily than his "panic-stricken running" in the beginning.

Even worse, when Henry feels secure about his badge of courage, and when his action wins unanimous praise, he develops a dangerous pride in himself and superiority to his fellow soldiers. He soon believes himself to be "a man of experience". He freely begins to condemn other men, even denouncing the commander of the forces. He is self-satisfied with his public image now. [Poet and critic] Mordecai Marcus criticizes this pride because it is not "an intelligent and self-willed motive," stating that "the dominance of pride in Henry's successful fighting casts convincing doubts on the thesis that Henry now acts with self-willed courage".

Lacking a Cause to Guide Him

Furthermore, Henry's motivation is distorted because of his lack of a righteous inducement. Wolford, having surveyed the historical theories of heroism, summarizes that heroism basically constitutes fulfillment of one's obligation. This novel, though stripped of certain referents to historical facts, is generally accepted as a description of a battle in the Civil War. However, throughout his meditation, Henry never anticipates himself in the cause of liberating slaves. There is only one reference to African Americans in the novel, and that reference is ironic, for, as [critic] Amy Kaplan observes, by having the African American teamster dance upon a cracker box and then lose the attention of other soldiers, Crane demotes the glorious cause of "emancipation" to "a form of entertainment". As a result, as [scholar] Donald Pease observes, not having any "noble" cause to direct his combative impulses, Henry has to pursue "personal aggrandizement". Though this lack of moral direction poses no problem for some theorists such as Oliver Wendell Holmes, Jr., it is just what Crane seems to attack in this novel. Through the exhibition of Henry's early cowardice and diffidence as well as the later exposure of his absurd courage, Crane proves that "without any abstract moral principle to organize and legitimize his behavior, he [Henry] feels compelled to develop an ethos of fear as his basis for unique personality".

Fleming Acts on Animal Rage

After exposing Henry's problem with a dutiful motivation, Crane then questions the quality of Henry's courage. On the second day of fighting, Henry appears completely different from the boy he had been the day before. He seems very brave, risking his life to carry the flag and running in the lead. In light of these apparently heroic deeds, some critics believe that Henry achieves maturation through fighting. However, others see the courage he exhibits on the second day differently. Horsford, for example, contends that it is by no means better than his cowardice in his initial running because it consists of unreasonable "rage". . . .

Along with this irrational element in Henry's courage, [scholar Harold] Beaver also notes a quality of animalism: "Man is out of control: that is the burden of Crane's message". Through numerous examples of animal imagery, Crane succeeds in conveying that humanity has degenerated to animalism in war which is supposed to be heroic. [Critic] Winifred Lynsky asserts that through the use of powerful imagery Crane presents a battlefield of "un-reason" and demonstrates that "the powerful and insensate forces of war are meaningless in the sense that [they] are irrational and sub-human". . . .

Human Plight Diminished by the Environment

Last but not least important, Crane proves the stupidity of Henry's courage by exposing its futility. Crane always enjoins interest in man's relationship with his environment. Many of his characters are so vulnerable that they become victims of their surroundings without any personal awareness of their plight. Henry is an example of this situation. According to [critic] Peter Shaw, the opening sentence of the novel, which supplies the setting of the story, determines the ironic tone focussed on military matters and foreshadows a want of any heroism or encouragement in the latter part of the novel:

> The cold passed reluctantly from the earth, and the retiring fogs revealed an army stretched out on the hills, resting. As the landscape changed from brown to green, the army awakened, and began to tremble with eagerness at the noise of rumors.

In this picture, nature dominates man. More active than man, its cold "pass[es]," its fogs "reveal" and its landscape "change[s]." Probably, it also wakens the soldiers with its sounds. The only action that man takes by himself is to "tremble." Through this portrait, Crane seems to reduce man to a meaningless point against a vast backdrop. To enhance this effect, Crane deliberately strips the names from the characters he soon introduces as "the youth," "the tall soldier," "the loud soldier" or "the tattered man." He also refuses to divulge the identity of the army so that readers know the soldiers only as "blue-clothed men", or, if more precise, as recruits or veterans. Therefore, as Shaw observes, "in the scheme of things, the individual man is but part of an insignificant and undifferentiated mass. His largest, most heroic actions are merely lilliputian exhausting struggles in an indifferent, purposeless universe".

Marcus evidently agrees with Shaw by regarding the major irony in this novel to be Henry's conception of himself as important, for later revelation of the insignificance of both himself and his regiment denigrates his ostentation. After Henry ensures that his fellow soldiers do not have any suspicion about his wound, his self-pride soon swells. He believes that he has grown out of his inexperience and even hails himself as "the chosen of gods" who is "doomed to greatness". He is proud of the way he and his regiment have fought. However, the commander's evaluation of his men which Henry accidentally overhears destroys his self-image, for in the commander's eyes, these soldiers are like "mule drivers" or "mud diggers", whereas the soldiers deem themselves to have fought like the "devil" or "hell-roosters". Henry cannot help feeling startled when he suddenly learns that he is "insignificant". The regiment, as Crane describes, is "like a cart involved in mud and muddle". Naturalist critics will readily translate this description to mean that man is trapped by his environment. Charles Child Walcutt, recognizing Crane's efforts to set man's insignificance against his mighty environment, comments that the merit of this novel lies not only in the exposure of Henry's delusions, but, more importantly, in the fact that "the insanely grotesque and incongruous world ... [where] the movement is blind or frantic, the leaders are selfish, the goals are inhuman" deludes him.

Henry thus miserably realizes the futility of his courage. Even worse, he sees it only occasionally. Henry in fact is rather conscious of his environment, but his perception is not often valid. When his suspicion that he may run away from the battle worries him, even a mere house looks "ominous" and the woods "formidable". Then, when his worry does not materialize, the landscape no longer threatens him. Later, when his regiment is unable to advance, he "imagine[s] the universe to be against him", while at the end of the novel, after a temporary victory, Henry "smile[s], for he [sees] that the world [is] a world for him". Henry's ever-changing attitudes ultimately cast doubt on the validity of his last thought in the novel, causing many readers to question whether he has matured at all. [Critic] Darryl Hattenhauer, for instance, believes that Crane keeps his ironic tone until the very end of the novel because the apparently optimistic ending is a "pseudo presentation". Hattenhauer further illustrates his point by calling attention to the novel's last image—the sun, for which the usual connotation of hopefulness is undermined by a previous image of the sun. The sun, earlier in the novel "like a wafer," has no more reliability than Henry's perception.

The Purposeful Unreality of War in *The Red Badge of Courage*

James B. Colvert

James B. Colvert is a now-retired professor of literature at the University of Georgia. He has written a biography of Stephen Crane as well as the introductions to collections of Crane's work and scholarly essays on The Red Badge of Courage. *Colvert has also served on the editorial board of the Stephen Crane Society.*

In the viewpoint that follows, Colvert remarks that the initial reviewers of The Red Badge of Courage *were quick to identify it with the realist movement that was then in fashion. Colvert claims, however, that while Crane's examination of the grim life of soldiering (especially among lower-class volunteers) and the unpleasant nature of warfare tie him closely to his realist colleagues, his imagery and descriptive techniques anticipate the impressionist movement in literature that was soon to take hold with the advent of works by authors such as Joseph Conrad and Ford Madox Ford. According to Colvert, Crane's unusual imagery and unique metaphors—confined to the limited perception of the main character, Henry Fleming—still convinced readers that Crane presented warfare in all its ugliness. But Colvert insists that the dreamlike qualities Crane invoked through Fleming's emotional responses to his surroundings were designed to make the war seem "unreal"—that is, not objectively real but only glimpsed through the fevered imagination of the character.*

A few months after the publication of *The Red Badge of Courage* in the early fall of 1895, Stephen Crane was famous on both sides of the Atlantic as the author of the most

James B. Colvert, "Unreal War in *The Red Badge of Courage*," *War, Literature, and the Arts: An International Journal of the Humanities*, 1999, pp. 35–47. Copyright © 1999 James B. Colvert. Reproduced by permission of the author.

realistic war novel in our literature. Most of its first reviewers, unaware that the twenty-four-year-old writer had never been closer to a battlefield than the parade ground of his military prep school, assumed that *Red Badge* was, as the *Saturday Review* noted in April, 1896, "not unnaturally . . . the work of a man of more than middle age who had been under fire in the great Civil War in America, and simply recorded the vivid impressions of actual experience." The writer took this "extraordinary instance" as "another proof of the fact that the imagination can enter into and realize the actualities of life so vividly and deeply as to surpass in realism the records of experience." The journalist-novelist Harold Frederic, aware that its author had never seen real war and intrigued by what he felt to be the compelling authority of the book, tested this claim for the power of the imagination in a somewhat elaborate experiment. Rereading the "renowned" battle descriptions of such "big men" as [Leo] Tolstoy, [Émile] Zola, [Victor] Hugo, and [Prosper] Merimée, he found to his "surprise" that *Red Badge* made those great writers, all veterans of the real thing, seem "all wrong." Crane had bested them as a realist, Frederic suggested, precisely *because* he had never seen war. The "actual sight of battle," he theorized, "has some dynamic quality in it which overwhelms and crushes the literary faculty in the observer. At best, he gives us a conventional account of what happened . . . not what he really saw, but what all his reading has taught him that he must have seen." Like many of the novel's early readers, [Lieutenant-Colonel] T.W. Higginson marveled that Crane was "able to go behind [the stories of old soldiers], and give an account of their [lives], not only more vivid than they themselves have ever given, but more accurate."

Clearly, the book's purported realism was the main thing to these reviewers. A few hinted that they were aware that much of the feeling of the reality in *Red Badge* was attributable to Crane's vivid representations of his hero's psychological response to war rather than to the facts and conditions of war per se, an insight that anticipates a major premise of later criticism. [Nineteenth-century novelist] Nancy Huston Banks came very close to discovering the radical significance of this focus on Henry Fleming's interior life. "There is virtually but one figure, [Henry Fleming]," Banks wrote, "and his sensations and observations during the conflict fill the volume with thoughts and images as unreal as a feverish dream," an observation not intended, incidentally, as a compliment to Crane's art, so strong was her presumption that he had tried and failed to picture the battlefield as it really was.

The reviewer who came closest to discovering how important this mode of the "feverish dream" is for the basic design of *Red Badge* was George Wyndham, a veteran [of the British army] who had experienced the harrowing reality of the battlefield in his campaigning in Egypt as an officer in the Coldstream Guards. In his brilliant review, Wyndham anticipated more fully than any other contemporary critic the fundamental premises of twentieth-century criticism of *Red Badge*. To this astute reader, Crane's realism was unmistakably centered in its representation of his hero's mental life, and to Wyndham this was a virtue, not a fault, as it was to Banks. Henry Fleming, he wrote, "super-sensitive to every pinprick of sensation" is "a delicate meter of emotion and fancy," registering "waves of feeling [that] take exaggerated curves[,] and hallucination [that haunts] the brain." In all his battlefield descriptions and reports, Wyndham noted, Crane "confines himself only to such things as that youth heard and saw, and, of these, only to such as influenced his emotions."

A Highly Subjective View of War

Wyndham's insight into the wide-ranging effects of Crane's ingenious use of an extremely limited third-person point of view, one of the several features that mark the novel's radical originality, has been fully explored by such modern critics as

J.C. Levenson, Frank Bergon, Jean Cazemajou, Sergio Perosa, and James Nagel, to name a few of the best. By screening out the objective world that is the focus of traditional war narratives, this powerful, innovative device gives full play to Henry's distorted and sometimes hallucinatory interpretation of the things he sees, or thinks he sees, on the battlefield. The "real" war, in this narrative arrangement, is Henry's fantastic, incoherent visions of things and events engendered by his acute mental distress. The keenness of Wyndham's appreciation for the expressive power of Crane's narrative method and his superb use of striking images and metaphors to depict his hero's psychological turmoil is attested by the critic's own highly descriptive language:

> [T]o read these pages is in itself an experience of breathless, lambent detonating life. So brilliant and detached are the images evoked that like illuminated bodies actually seen, they leave their fever-bright phantasms floating before the brain. . . . The book is full of sensuous impressions that leap out from the picture: of gestures, attitudes, grimaces, that flash into portentous definition, like faces from the climbing clouds of nightmare. . . . It leaves, in short, such indelible traces as are left by the actual experience of war.

No one has described more clearly or succinctly the essential characteristic of the innovative realism of *Red Badge*. The war writings of Zola, [Wilbur F.] Hinman, [John William] De-Forest, and Tolstoy, which have been thoroughly combed for parallels of plot and characters, images, and descriptive details that might account for Crane's apparent military expertise, belong obviously to a different order of narrative. He was undoubtedly much indebted in various ways to these writers and others, to Tolstoy for the uses of irony, to [Rudyard] Kipling for hints about tone and color, and, as [scholar] Stanley Wertheim has demonstrated, to several earlier Civil War writers for certain conventional plot devices and information about equipment, training, and marching. But the significance of these influences seems relatively slight considered in the context of Wyndham's brilliant description of Crane's impressively original method and style.

Imposing Realism on Crane's Novel

Oddly, after laying out his exemplary interpretive scheme, Wyndham succumbed like many readers then and later to the notion that *Red Badge* is a classic instance of normative realism, a lapse that demonstrates that even the most independent-minded critic is not altogether immune to biases imposed by established contemporary literary norms (or by the critic's historical perception of such norms). A minor fault in the book, he wrote, is that the author's overemphasis on "the sharp, crashing of rifles" neglects the real sound of a bullet, its "long chromatic whine defining [its] invisible arc in the air, and [its] fretful snatch a few feet from the listener's head."

The standard of realism Wyndham tacitly invokes in this momentary lapse in insight is commonly encountered in a century of writing about *Red Badge*. Even the astute [Crane scholar] John Berryman seems to have thought of it occasionally as a naturalistic representation of war, as when he observes in passing that "some authority has got to be allowed [Crane], and identified, since professional military men were surprised to learn that he was not one." A scholar writing more recently thinks that this authority derives at least partly from Crane's "mental reconstruction" in early 1893 of the actual plans of attacks and counterattacks at Chancellorsville and of Stonewall Jackson's "brilliant fifteen-mile flanking action"—an assumption that seems hopelessly irrelevant to what we actually find in the text of *Red Badge*. Even so notable a critic as Harold Bloom has lately declared that any reader "who has gone through warfare from 1895 to the present could testify to the uncanny accuracy of [Crane's] representation of battle."

Crane's Imaginative History

As I have obviously been suggesting, such views of *Red Badge* lead us in a wrong direction. They implicitly rationalize Henry's poetic madness and impose upon Crane's book the clarity and order of such realistic accounts of war as Tolstoy's wonderful memoirs of the siege of Sebastopol, or Joseph Kirklands's vivid and authentic *The Captain of Company K*, or William DeForest's stark account of the battlefields of Louisiana. But as I have noted, the purposes, methods, and imaginative groundings of these and other nineteenth-century realists of war were radically different from Crane's, and their books are probably not as important in the history of his novel as historians (including the present writer) have sometimes claimed. The true imaginative history of *Red Badge* begins, I believe, with the wonderfully fanciful Sullivan County sketches Crane wrote in the early nineties, eerie anecdotal pieces about the farcical adventures of four men fishing, hunting, and camping in the wilds of Sullivan County, New York. All of these "little grotesque tales of the woods," as Crane once referred to them, were written before 1892, and several were published in the summer of that year in the *New York Tribune*. By 1893 Crane felt that he had outgrown them and tried to repudiate them as objectionably "clever" shortly before he began writing *Red Badge* in the spring:

> It seemed to me [he wrote Lily Brandon Munroe (a lady friend), referring to the tales] that there must be something more in life than to sit and cudgel one's brains for clever and witty expedients. So I developed all alone a little creed of art which I thought was a good one. Later I discovered that my creed was identical with the one of [William Dean] Howells and [Hamlin] Garland and in this way I became involved in the beautiful war between those who say that art is man's substitute for nature and that we are the most successful in art when we approach the nearest to nature and truth, and those who say well, I don't know what they say.

At this time Crane probably knew in the casual way in which he always entertained theories, literary or otherwise, that Garland's "creed of art" ("Veritism") supported in principle what he was about to do in *Red Badge,* but his language suggests that he was thinking vaguely of realism as most literary-minded people (reviewers like Banks, for example) understood it in the mid-nineties. In any case, it is hard to see how he might have supposed that the radical and seminal book he would write over the next few months was in any way related in either theory or practice to Howellsian realism. What seems clear, despite his disclaimer, is that Crane never actually abandoned the motifs, compositional patterns, and narrative method he developed in the Sullivan County tales. The characters, themes, and above all the images and metaphors of the haunted Sullivan County landscape he discovered in writing these broadly drawn sketches served as a rich resource for much of his later war writing, not only in *Red Badge, The Little Regiment,* and *Wounds in the Rain,* but in some of the newspaper reports of real war he filed from the battlefields of Greece and Cuba. In these early sketches are the familiar animistic landscapes, with their menacing mountains, glowering red suns and flickering twilight shadows, their dark caves, night-cloaked mysteries, and—in dramatic ironic contrast—their sunny vales, dappled blue skies, fair fields, and other images of pastoral benignity.

The Landscape Invested with the Character's Emotions

The unnamed hero of the tales is the outrageously conceited, almost anonymous, "little man" (occasionally addressed as "Billie" by his comrades), who is clearly the fictional ancestor of the apprehensive and vainglorious Henry Fleming of *Red Badge.* Like Henry, the little man is beguiled by impossible heroic dreams, and again like Henry is victimized by his almost hysterical fear of what he characteristically perceives as the dark, threatening powers of an alien landscape, the rugged, disordered wilderness of Sullivan County. Like his descendant Henry, the little man detects in the fields, hills and streams living presences, intimations of mystery and threat, manifestations, as he perceives them, of the dark powers of an inscrutable nature. A looming mountain (in "The Mesmeric Mountain") seems to exude a brooding malevolence, like the menace of the low-browed hills in the famous opening paragraphs of *Red Badge*. Fishing the depths of a lazy, sleeping lake, the little man uneasily discerns "millions of fern branches [that] quivered and hid mysteries," just as Henry, crossing a stream with his regiment, detects in its black waters the gaze of uncanny "white bubble eyes." Approaching a forest, Henry fears that he "might be fearfully assaulted from the caves of the lowering woods" and thrills with unease when he sees dark columns of troops on the slopes of distant hills crawling like monsters from the "caves of night." In "Across the Covered Pit," a "gloomy and forbidding" cave challenges an amateur spelunker "to tread its dark mysteries and explore its unknown recesses," and the animistic cavern in "Four Men in a Cave" strikes terror into the hearts of the little man and his comrades.

In both the sketches and the novel, the hero perceives in the landscape baffling ambiguities. Its apparent malignity can dissolve instantly into aspects that seem benign and sympathetic, serene and pastoral. The surface of the lake that conceals mysteries in its murky depths is dappled with merry sunbeams, a contradiction that suggest a fundamental disorder in the very scheme of things, a constantly recurring motif in the fantasy world Henry conjures up in the novel. In one famous paragraph Henry, looking up from the desperate work of a firefight, "felt a flash of astonishment at the blue, pure sky and the sun gleamings on the trees and fields" and wonders "that Nature had gone tranquilly on with her golden process in the midst of so much devilment". His world—shadowy, menacing, monstrous, but also cheerful, pastoral, and inno-cent—shifts meanings with the ebb and flow of his emotions, and mirrors back to him his disquieting sense of a pervasive moral and psychological uncertainty.

Tainted Objectivity

Although discontinuous, incoherent fantasy is fundamental to the structure of *Red Badge*, Crane's narrative style occasionally presents another kind of perceptual deviation. Hallucination may seem on occasion to give way to its opposite, an un-clouded perception of detailed objective fact, but actually there is very little objectivity in *Red Badge*, not even in those passages that have sometimes been cited as models of natural-istic description. An example is the much-noted description of the corpse Henry encounters in a little cathedral-like bower, notable for its flat delineation of a number of gruesome de-tails:

> He was being looked at by a dead man who was seated with his back against a columnlike tree. The corpse was dressed in a uniform that once had been blue, but was now faded to a melancholy shade of green. The eyes, staring at the youth, had changed to the dull hue to be seen on the side of a dead fish. The mouth was open. Its red had changed to an appall-ing yellow. Over the gray skin of the face ran little ants. One was trundling some sort of a bundle along the upper lip.

But even at this crucial moment, when Henry's perception seems to break the boundaries of its normally exclusive inferi-ority and to see things in the unfiltered light of objective real-ity, we detect a certain disordering hysteria. The exaggerated clarity of the image, with the usual shadowy ambiguity mo-mentarily suspended to permit the seen thing to leap to the mind in a fullness of unqualified detail, suggests strong psy-chological tensions. In the middle ground between subjective distortion and obsessive discrimination of detail we may ex-pect to find a persuasive objectivity, but we may also be aware, as [Crane scholar] Donald Pease notes, that what is represented in *Red Badge* is never wholly stable, never wholly fixed in a coherent context. A sudden change in Henry's emotional state may instantly return any momentary perception of truth to a state of eerie unreality.

This mode of representation creates a world far removed from those of conventional realists. If Crane was looking for compositional models in the memoirs of soldiers in the copies of *Century Magazine* he borrowed from his friend C.W. Linson, he very likely saw Pvt. David L. Thompson's memorable eye-witness description of the large-scale deployment of Federal forces on September 14, 1862, for the Battle of Antietam. From a position on a slope overlooking the valley of Middletown lying far below, Thompson observed long columns of Federal troops as they crossed the valley and disappeared over the farther ridge:

> . . . backward and downward, across the valley and up the farther slope, [a column] stretched with scarcely a gap, every curve and zigzag of the way defined more sharply by its somber presence. Here, too, on all the distant portions of the line, motion was imperceptible, but could be inferred from the casual glint of sunlight on a musket barrel miles away. It was 3 o'clock when we resumed our march, turning our backs upon the beautiful, impressive picture—each column a monstrous, crawling, blue-black snake, miles long, quilted with the silver slant of muskets at a "shoulder," its sluggish tail writhing slowly up over the distant eastern ridge, its bruised head weltering in the roar and smoke upon the crest above. . . .

We can easily imagine Crane's fascination with the unusual perspective in the description. Such visual oddities are evident everywhere in his writing, especially in *Red Badge*, as in his curious image, to cite a single example, of Henry's view of the harried movements of distant artillery: "Once he saw a tiny battery go dashing along the line of the horizon. The tiny riders were beating the tiny horses". But we can also imagine quite as easily that he would have found Thompson's vivid description useless as a guide for composition in *Red Badge*. Implicit in Thompson's account, of course, is normal perception; his description gives no hint, as does Crane's representation of Henry's deviant perception, that distance actually diminishes the size of observed objects. Crane's imagery seems closer to the distorted perceptions of the little man in the Sullivan County sketches than to any model of realism he might have encountered in contemporary war literature. Thompson's realistic description of the snake-like column of infantry becomes in *Red Badge* Henry's hallucinatory perception of monsters, the "red and green dragons" of his haunted imagination:

> When the sunrays at last struck full and mellowingly upon the earth, the youth saw that the landscape was streaked with two long, thin, black columns which disappeared on the brow of a hill in front and rearward vanished in a wood. They were like two serpents crawling from the cavern of the night.

The unreality of war in *Red Badge* becomes even clearer when we imagine the effect of substituting one of Joseph Kirkland's realistic descriptions of an artillery action in *The Captain of Company K* for one of Crane's in *Red Badge*. This is Kirkland's account:

> [A] flash in the opposite woods sent across the cornfield a slight gleam visible in spite of the sunshine. Soon followed the roar of a distant field-piece, and, almost at the same instant with the sound, the shriek of a near shell passing over.... [T]hen among the trees behind ... there was another great bang as the shell burst; then a humming, as of a hundred gigantic bees, from the fragments of the shell as they flew through the air.... The men dropped flat down as if they had been struck by lightning. It seemed impossible for human nature to stand up before and beneath the yelling, flying beast. Fargeon [the company commander] ... felt

113

as if he could not hug mother earth closely enough—he would have liked to dig a hole, with his nails, to hide in.

Such sustained clarity of perception is impossible for Henry Fleming. The careful delineation of time and space—the observer's detection of the flash and roar of the distant gun, the slightly delayed passing of the screaming shell, the following explosion in the trees to the rear, then the deadly hum of the scattering shrapnel—is grounded in a rational perspective totally alien to the mercurial mind of Crane's hero. In the context of Kirkland's rational perception, the figurative characterization of the shell as a "yelling, flying beast" seems, like Thompson's metaphor of the snake, merely illustrative. . . .

Purposefully Impressionistic

It has not always been clear to readers from William Dean Howells' time to our own that war in *Red Badge* is *necessarily* unreal, that its unreality, as reflected in Henry's distorted visions, is in fact central to the novel's argument. Howells' notion that the dream-like evocation of war is Crane's unsuccessful attempt to bring the battlefield into the common light of day is proof that he did not understand the book. He believed, in accordance with his doctrinaire theory of realism, that Crane's metaphoric war is evidence that he "lost himself in a whirl of wild guesses at the fact from the ground of insufficient witness," that his figures and images of war are symptoms of "an art failing with material to which it could not render an absolute devotion from an absolute knowledge." Howells tried to show the book's failure by referencing it to the criteria of naive literary realism, and readers from Nancy Banks to Harold Bloom have tried to validate it by the same measure. Perhaps one reason is that the overall feeling of realism readers get from its vivid imagery, its ironic deflation of the heroic ideal, and its uncanny insights into the psychology of the suffering hero compels them to restore unconsciously to his brooding fantasies the reality they distort.

But the book, after all, is about the moral consequences of Henry's flawed view of himself and the world, and in *Red Badge* that world is war. Crane's realism, newer than Howells's and Garland's and already pointing toward the expressionism of the approaching new century, is in its credible portrayal of Henry's distorting moral and psychological anguish. Howell's sense that Crane's "floundering" attempt to portray real war resulted in merely "a huddled and confused effect" ironically verified its success. For in the design of Crane's great novel, wrought consciously or not, war could not have been anything but unreal.

Full Metal Jacket Surpasses Crane's War Realism

James A. Stevenson

James A. Stevenson was an associate professor of history at Dalton State College in Georgia until his retirement in 2006.

Director Stanley Kubrick's 1987 film Full Metal Jacket *deals with the training of U.S. Marines for combat during the Vietnam War. As Stevenson contends in the following viewpoint, Kubrick shows how the military takes raw recruits and brutalizes them until they acquire the skills and mindset to become vicious killers. Stevenson notes how Stephen Crane's* The Red Badge of Courage *also contends with the issue of changing timid and boastful volunteers into battle-hardened veterans who understand the grim reality of war. In Stevenson's opinion, however, Crane's depicted transformation is less harsh than Kubrick's. Crane's Henry Fleming expresses some individuality and retains the ability to criticize his superiors even after acquiescing to regimental discipline, Stevenson argues. Kubrick, on the other hand, reveals how the military sadistically intimidates its trainees with the intent of removing individualism and instilling strict obedience to orders. Once engaged in combat, Kubrick's and Crane's characters also show marked differences, according to Stevenson: Henry Fleming feels pride in the self-esteem he achieves through victory; Kubrick's marines simply feel the hollow void of killing and the madness of warfare.*

There is one characteristic of *Full Metal Jacket* which virtually all film critics have overlooked. And, although they have touched on the realism beneath *Jacket*'s satire, they have not appreciated how completely realistic the bootcamp scenes

James A. Stevenson, "Beyond Stephen Crane: *Full Metal Jacket*," *Literature/Film Quarterly*, vol. 16, no. 4, 1988, pp. 238–243. Copyright © 1988 Salisbury State College. Reproduced by permission.

are. But, most importantly, what really has eluded the critics is Stanley Kubrick's grand sense of the ironic. Kubrick and his fellow screenwriters, Michael Herr and Gustave Hasford, did not just create a film with ironic scenes and flashes of the sardonic. They constructed a twentieth century parody of a famous nineteenth-century story, *The Red Badge of Courage*. Their movie is a marvelous antidote to that classic book and subsequent [1951] film produced by Gottfried Reinhardt and directed by John Huston.

A Parody of the *Red Badge* Model

In sequence after sequence, Kubrick's film parallels Stephen Crane's "realistic" war story. Indeed, Kubrick's satire makes *Jacket*'s script more realistic than Crane's much acclaimed account. This is due to the fact that *Jacket*'s satire springs out of the very nature of recruit training and war. It is not satire to show Marine recruits hugging their rifles and skipping the childhood prayer of "Now I lay me down to sleep . . ." for a bedtime recitation of the Marine rifle creed, "My Rifle":

> Without me my rifle is useless. Without my rifle, I am useless I must fire my rifle true. I must shoot straighter than my enemy who is trying to kill me. I must shoot him before he shoots me. I will.

> Before God I swear this creed. My rifle and myself are defenders of my country. We are the masters of our enemy. We are saviours of my life. So be it . . . until there is no enemy . . . but peace. Amen.

Verging on idolatry, this prayer is an affirmation of killing one's earthly neighbors, not of loving or forgiving them. And it is something that the Corps, not Kubrick, Herr or Hasford, dreamed up. Quite frankly, the incongruity of praying to the Prince of Peace for help in killing one's enemies is too ludicrous for most sane minds to bear. Crane's soldiers, in contrast, have no bloodlust prayers to inspire their will to fight, but *Jacket*, nevertheless, drives many of its points home by following the model of *The Red Badge of Courage*.

As *Jacket* opens and scenes reflecting both the film and book versions of *The Red Badge of Courage* begin to unfold, we are treated to recruits beginning their training for war; we hear a narration by the new Henry, i.e., Joker (all Marine recruits were given nicknames by their Drill Instructor, Sergeant Hartman); we see impatient recruits fighting among themselves; we hear unbloodied Marines in a scene of bravado and bragging that is disrupted by an enemy attack and, of course, sudden doubts of courage; we watch periodic discussions of life and war by the troopers; we see a bloody attack on a position, not by a courageous regiment of men, but by a squad of frightened human beings; we witness the conquest of the enemy position (held not by a regiment of Rebels, but by one female sniper); we see the men looking at their defeated and fallen enemy and talking about their triumph; we hear Rafterman give Joker a medal of "ugly" for bravely killing the helpless, wounded sniper; and, finally, we see the film end with the victorious Marines marching off the screen.

Training to Be Killers

Crane's version of similar events is more benign. Indeed, when Henry's mother sends her son to war, she warns him of "bad men," but barely realizes that the worst influence is the army itself:

> An' allus be careful an' choose yer comp'ny. There's lots of bad men in the army, Henry. The army makes 'em wild, and they like nothing better than the job of leading off a young feller like you . . . a-learning 'em to drink and swear.

Going beyond Crane, *Jacket* reveals that it is the "army" that really "makes 'em." This is demonstrated when, after weeks of listening to Sergeant Hartman's foul rhetoric, Joker and Cowboy are assigned to clean the head (toilet area), and a desensitized Joker asks a desensitized Cowboy for a date with Cowboy's sister in this degrading exchange:

Joker: I want to slip my tubesteak into your sister. What'll you take in trade?

Cowboy: What have you got?

Then, too, when Crane's recruits get on each other's nerves, they react as individuals angry at other individuals. Irritated at the empty bragging of the "loud soldier" (Tom Wilson), Henry is moved to chastise him with the remark: "Oh shucks! said the youth. You ain't the bravest man in the world, are you?" But Henry's twentieth century counterpart, Joker, confronts his inept comrade-in-arms with more than mere words. After the entire recruit platoon has viciously constrained Gomer with towel-en-cased bars of soap, Joker contributes the final terrible blows and leaves a whimpering Gomer several clicks closer to a mental breakdown.

Former Marines can empathize with such bootcamp scenes because they realize that the whole theory and practice of Marine Corps bootcamp is predicated on the calculated exercise of terror/sadism. When *Jacket* depicts boot training as so dehumanizing that it drives Gomer insane, it is more realistic than satirical. In fact, the recruit, who is driven insane by training practices, only symbolizes what such training ought to produce. Indeed, it is surprising that more recruits are not driven mad. Perhaps, most men are spared because they can be trained into insensitivity at a point which stops just short of madness and veers them off from a more serious emotional collapse. In other words, they do not reach the epitome toward which their brutal boot training drives them, but they come damn close.

Destroying Individualism

In Kubrick's film, the practice of punishing all for the mistakes of one (Gomer) causes the entire platoon to trap and mercilessly beat the hapless Gomer. This is exactly what Drill

Instructor Hartman has goaded them into doing. And the true irony of this common bootcamp practice (mass punishment) is that the ideal of "one for all and all for one" is attained by having "all" gang up on "one." Crane, on the other hand, has his protagonist become a part of the unit by the much more traditional method of drills, parades, inspections, and boredom. "He had grown to regard himself merely as part of a vast blue demonstration. . . . Also, he was drilled and drilled and reviewed, and drilled and drilled and reviewed". Crane, in short, depicts the loss of individuality as more benevolent and more useful than does Kubrick. Although Henry, at one point, feels trapped by the "iron laws of tradition" and the "moving box" of the marching regiment, he has not lost his personality. Shortly after his recruit training, he can still envision addressing his comrades and persuading them that the "generals were idiots," and that they must break ranks to prevent themselves from being "killed like pigs".

Independent thinking certainly is not a hallmark of Marine boot training, and *Jacket* demonstrates this in its opening scenes of recruits having their heads shaved. And, while Crane can picture his soldiers as no less than the biological equivalent of "pigs," Kubrick exposes us to the painful reality of individuals treated as less than pigs. On the journey to Marine "manhood," recruits not only lose their hair, but their self-respect. That, of course, is the goal which a shouting Sergeant Hartman strives to attain,

> If you ladies leave my island, . . . you will be a minister of death, praying for war. But until that day you are pukes! You're the lowest form of life on Earth. You are not even human f--king beings! You are nothing but unorganized grabasstic pieces of amphibian shit!

No equivalent speech can be found in Crane's realism. The angry lieutenant who strikes a lagging Henry with the flat of his sword is less like Sergeant Hartman and more like one of those tough but fair drill sergeants who populate conventional

American war movies. *Jacket* breaks this mode and puts the lie to the basic training clichés that have recruits enjoying themselves, talking without permission or taking their drill instructor behind the barracks for a man-to-man fist fight. While one may challenge Sergeant John Wayne or Richard Widmark, no one challenges a real-life drill instructor. Whoever appears to do so doubletimes himself and his platoon into deep shit. Illustrating this, Hartman's discovery of Gomer's jelly doughnut results in the ordeal of extra physical training for everyone but Gomer. The book on which *Jacket* is based, *The Short-Timers*, makes the logic behind this method of obedience training explicit:

> Now, whenever Leonard [Gomer] makes a mistake, Sergeant Gerheim [Hartman] does not punish [Gomer]. He punishes the whole platoon. He excludes [Gomer] from the punishment. While [Gomer] rests, we do squat-thrusts and side-straddle hops, many, many of them.

Neither Crane's book nor Huston's movie confronts such realities as this time-honored method of mass intimidation. And *Jacket* touches on more truths when it pokes a big hole in the "great buddies" myth by having a finally demented Gomer blow a hole in his drill instructor's chest with a "full metal jacket" (i.e., 7.62 bullet).

How Recruits Ponder the Realities of War

As *Jacket* approaches its war scenes, the parallels with Crane's novel and Huston's film become more striking. When tent-mates Jocker, Payback, Chili, and Rafterman discuss combat, the unbloodied Joker's bragging is reminiscent of Henry and Wilson's intemperate speech before a thoughtful Jim Conklin.

> *Joker*: I am f--king bored to death, man. I gotta get back in the shit. I ain't heard a shot fired in anger in weeks.

> *Payback*: Joker's so tough he'd eat the boogers out of a dead man's nose . . . then ask for seconds.

Scene from Stanley Kubrick's 1987 film Full Metal Jacket. *Kubrick's film goes beyond Crane's realistic portrayal of war to capture an even grittier picture of the brutality and madness that soldiers experience in modern warfare.* Warner Bros./The Kobal Collection/ The Picture Desk, Inc.

> *Joker (in John Wayne voice)*: Listen up, pilgrim. A day without blood is like a day without sunshine.
>
> *Payback*: He's never been in the shit. It's hard to talk about it, man. It's like on [Operation] Hastings. . . . You know he's never been in the shit, 'cause he ain't got the stare.

Similarly, Crane has his pre-battle tested tentmates, Henry, Wilson, and Conklin, stating,

> *Henry*: Well, . . . I'd rather do anything 'most than go tramping 'round the country all day doing no good to nobody and jest tiring ourselves out.
>
> *Wilson*: So would I . . . It ain't right. I tell you if anybody with any sense was a-runnin' this army it—
>
> *Conklin*: Oh shut up! . . . You little fool. You little damn' cuss. You ain't had that there coat and them pants on for six months, and yet you talk as if—

In both war stories, the bragging terminates when the shells fly close. Hence, characters, nearly a hundred years apart, react in timeless fear as lethal explosions threaten their existence.

> *Joker*: Hey, I hope they're just f--king with us. I ain't ready for this shit.

> *Stork*: Amen.

> To the youth [Henry] it was an onslaught of redoubtable dragons. He became like the man who lost his legs at the approach of the red and green monster. He waited in a sort of a horrified listening attitude. He seemed to shut his eyes and wait to be gobbled.

So, Joker and Henry share a desire to avoid the "shit," but they also share the experience of standing over and wondering about the deaths of fallen comrades. When Conklin dies at Henry's feet, Henry and the "tattered man" stand looking down at him, and the tattered man says,

> Well he was a reg'lar jim-dandy for nerve, wa'n't he ... A reg'lar jim-dandy ... I wonder where he got 'is stren'th from?

> The youth desired to screech out his grief. He was stabbed but his tongue lay dead in the tomb of his mouth.

Likewise, Joker and his buddies peer down at their fallen comrades, Lieutenant Touchdown and Hand Job, and try to extract some meaning from their bloody deaths:

> *T.H.E. Rock*: You're going home now.

> *Crazy Earl: Semper fi.*

> *Donolon*: We're mean marines, sir.

> *Eightball*: Go easy, bros.

Animal Mother: Better you than me.

Cowboy: Tough break for Hand Job. He was all set to get shipped out on a medical.

Joker: What was the matter with him?

Cowboy: He was jerkin' off ten times a day.

In their respective fallen soldier scenes, the essential difference between Kubrick, Herr, and Hasford's view of war and Crane's view of war is clearly evident. Crane's dialogue makes us aware of a tragic loss, but *Jacket*'s dialogue makes us aware of both loss and brutality.

Hollow Victory

With dialogue and visual imagery, *Jacket* becomes an anti-war movie by bringing the brutality of war into sharp focus. This accomplishment is most dramatically found in a comparison of the climactic battle scenes of the two works. While a crouching Henry waits to charge across a shell-splattered field, his lieutenant urges him onward: "Come on, yeh lunkhead! . . . Come on; We'll all get killed if we stay here. We've on'y got t' go across that lot. An' then—". So, shaking free of his lieutenant's clutch, Henry begins his reckless leadership of a death-defying attack with the shout. "Come on yerself, then". Henry charges, and he survives. Many of his buddies did not survive. And neither do several of Joker's friends when they seek to attack and kill the enemy sniper who has been baiting them by repeatedly wounding Eightball (leg, arm, foot, thigh). Ultimately, against Cowboy's orders, Doc Jay and, later, Animal Mother leave their protective wall to rush to the dying Eightball's assistance. Doc Jay and Eightball are killed, but the squad eventually charges the murderous sniper with the same fearful anxiety that Henry and his comrades exhibited in their attack on a protected Confederate regiment.

Cowboy: Okay, Listen up; No-Doze, Sutten, Donlon, Rock—you come with me, we'll take a look! The rest of you stay put and cover our ass; We may be coming back in a big hurry.

Joker: I'm going with you.

Rafterman: I'm coming too!

Cowboy: Okay. You all set.

Adlibs: Yeah!

Cowboy: Let's move out;

T.H.E. Rock: Let's do it!

The advance, only "across that lot," positions the squad for a final rush on the concealed sniper. Before that final leap to victory, however, Cowboy is killed.

When Henry's battered regiment at last captures the enemy's stronghold, his friend, Wilson, triumphantly wrenches a flag from the hands of a bullet-riddled, dying Confederate. And the victors immediately gang around various defiant, morose, good natured, and/or dejected prisoners. The men in blue, of course, are elated at being alive, and they are filled with self-congratulatory thoughts. To them, everything but living and victory seems superfluous. Comparable relief is depicted in *Jacket* when Joker, Rafterman, Donlon, T.H.E. Rock, and Animal Mother group around the dying fifteen-year-old Vietnamese sniper who has killed their buddies. As she lies suffering and praying, the squad members discuss their conquest and whether to leave or to kill their torn and bleeding prisoner. Finally, urged on by the others, a deeply troubled Joker shoots her with his pistol, and Rafterman says, "Joker . . . we're gonna have to put you up for the Congressional Medal of . . . Ugly!" Unlike Henry's triumph, however, Joker's victory is not only hollow but bitter and foul.

Man vs. Madman

As *Jacket* and the *Red Badge of Courage* reach their narrated denouements, Henry and Joker reflect on what their experiences have taught them. Henry's regiment, for instance, marches toward a river and "a golden ray of sun came through the hosts of leaden rain clouds." Against this hopeful symbol of nature returned to its proper place, the narrator voices Henry's proud thoughts, "He had been to touch the great death, and found that, after all, it was but the great death [and was for others]. He was a man". Joker also marches toward a river ("River of Perfumes"), but that night walk is made by a platoon of cynical Marines singing, not the "Battle Hymn of the Republic," but the more appropriate "Mickey Mouse." And they are not touched by a single ray of pure, innocent sunshine but are silhouetted against the raging inferno of a destroyed Hue. Thus, little of the spiritual touches Joker's final, earthy thoughts:

> My thoughts drift back to erect nipple wet dreams about Mary Jane Rottencrotch and the Great Homecoming F--k Fantasy. I am so happy that I am alive, in one piece and short. I'm in a world of shit . . . yes. But I am alive. And I am not afraid.

Although separated by almost a hundred years, the characters of Joker and Henry express two overwhelming similarities. They have braved their battles, and they are both still alive. The great dissimilarity between the messages which these two characters convey, however, is that Crane teaches us that war makes one a *man* while *Jacket* teaches us that war makes one a *madman*.

Echoing the novel and film versions of *The Red Badge of Courage* in so many of its scenes, *Full Metal Jacket* employs realism as satire and satire as realism. In the surreal world of sadistic drill instructors, elusive enemies, and death by the law of averages, everything—patriotism, honor, courage—is out of place. The gung ho colonel berating Joker put it this way: ". . . inside every gook there is an American trying to get out. It's a hardball world, son. We've gotta keep our heads until this peace craze blows over". Such ridiculous comments provide insights into a reality that Crane's solemnity cannot match. [Singer] Billy Joel has it right in his "Goodnight Saigon" lyrics on the bootcamp/war experience: "We met as soul mates/ On Parris Island/ We left as inmates/ From an asylum/ . . . We came in spastic/ Like tameless horses/ We left in plastic/ As numbered corpses . . ." And Kubrick, Herr, and Hasford have it right when they surpass Crane's version of realism. War and the training for war is a hell that only sarcasm and satire can truly capture.

Social Issues
in Literature

Contemporary
Perspectives on War

War Is Not an Innate Part of Human Nature

John Horgan

A former senior writer at Scientific American, *John Horgan is the director of the Center for Science Writings at the Stevens Institute of Technology in New Jersey.*

For centuries, philosophers, social critics, and other thinkers have assumed that warfare is an intrinsic part of human nature. But over time, the world has become more peaceful, not more war-like, asserts Horgan in the following viewpoint. Horgan maintains that this growing peacefulness is likely due to the advances of civilization—such as the implementation of broad communication technologies and the increasing numbers of stable states with impartial legal systems—that have led to greater interaction and strengthened interdependence among disparate nations. Horgan insists that humans must continue to work toward achieving global peace and dispel the notion that violence is inevitable, for only by countering this fatalistic view will people begin to accept that war is a solvable social ill and not an inescapable fate.

I taught "War and Human Nature" again [in fall 2008]. The course ponders the question, as my syllabus puts it, "Is war inevitable, or are peace and even universal disarmament possible?" During the first class, I posed that question to my undergraduate students, most of them engineering and science majors. Thirteen said no, peace is not possible, and four said yes, it is. At least one of those yeses, I'm pretty sure, was telling the teacher what he wanted to hear.

That pessimistic response no longer surprises me. Two years ago [in 2007]. I had my students ask classmates: "Will

John Horgan, "Countering Students' Fatalism Toward War," *Chronicle of Higher Education*, vol. 55, no. 31, April 10, 2009, pp. B10–B11. Copyright © 2009 by *The Chronicle of Higher Education*. Reprinted by permission of the author.

humans ever stop fighting wars, once and for all? Why or why not?" Of the 205 respondents, 185—more than 90 percent—replied no. The justifications were diverse: "We're naturally evil people." "People are always going to hate and try to destroy 'inferiors.'" "Monkeys fight with each other and because humans are animals, too, we follow that pattern." "Men are power-crazy and women are not in power." "People would just get bored with no war."

Even more disconcertingly, some of those who answered yes revealed in their explanations that they were actually pessimists: "Yes, because in the future the human species will unite to fight alien species." "Yes, but it will only happen under the same one religion, because one's beliefs are a driving force." "Yes, when someone (Korea) launches their nuclear weapon. Then we'll all stop messing with each other and keep it cool." "Yes. Humanity will end wars once everyone is killed."

"From this survey," one of my students wrote, "we can conclude that most college students have little faith in mankind."

A More Pessimistic World

Young people have less faith now than they did decades ago, if previous surveys are any guide. In 1987 the psychologist David Adams, of Wesleyan University, polled 126 students on whether "wars are inevitable because human beings are naturally aggressive." Only 33 percent of the students agreed with that statement, and only 40 percent believed that "war is intrinsic to human nature." The results resemble those obtained in similar surveys of 327 students in Finland in 1984 and of 5,000 students in 18 nations in 1969.

My students' pessimism reflects that of the general population. Over the past few years, I've taken every opportunity—on the Internet, during lectures, at conferences and parties, in restaurants and taxis—to ask people of all ages and backgrounds whether they think war will ever be abolished. More than nine people in 10 give me the same answer: War will never end.

The current wave of fatalism is all too understandable, given September 11 [2001] and its bloody sequelae, not to mention conflicts roiling the Middle East, Central Africa, and other troubled regions. As an old-fashioned liberal peacenik, however, I find fatalism toward warfare—especially among young people disturbing, because it has the potential to become a self-fulfilling belief. If you believe wars are inevitable, you are more likely to support hawkish politicians and policies. So, in my course, I try to get my pessimistic students to reconsider their views by exposing them to continuing investigations into warfare by anthropologists, archaeologists, political scientists, biologists, and others.

Violent Ancestry

That research seems, at first glance, to support a fatalistic view of warfare. As far back as scientists have looked into human prehistory, they have found evidence of lethal fighting. The anthropologist Lawrence Keeley, of the University of Illinois at Chicago, estimates that more than 90 percent of pre-state, tribal societies engaged in at least occasional warfare, and that many fought constantly. Tribal combat usually involved skirmishes and ambushes rather than pitched battles, but over time the fighting could produce mortality rates as high as 50 percent.

Those findings, the Harvard archaeologist Steven LeBlanc contends, demolish the claim of the 18th-century French philosopher Jean-Jacques Rousseau that before civilization, humans were "noble savages" living in harmony with one another and with nature. Primeval warfare, LeBlanc asserts, stemmed from a fierce, Malthusian [after a theory by economist Thomas Malthus] struggle for food and other resources. "Since the beginning of time," he writes, "humans have been unable to live in ecological balance. No matter where we happen to live on earth, we eventually outstrip the environment. This has always led to competition as a means of survival, and warfare has been the inevitable consequence of our ecological-demographic propensities."

Some scientists now trace warfare all the way back to the common ancestor we shared with chimpanzees, our closest genetic relatives. Beginning in the mid-1970s, researchers in Tanzania and elsewhere have observed male chimpanzees from the same troop banding together to patrol their territory; if they encounter a chimp from a different troop, the raiders beat him, often to death. Mortality rates from intergroup violence among chimpanzees, the Harvard anthropologist Richard Wrangham reports, are roughly comparable to rates observed among human hunter-gatherers.

"Chimpanzee-like violence preceded and paved the way for human war," Wrangham says, "making modern humans the dazed survivors of a continuous, five-million-year habit of lethal aggression." He contends that male primates "evolved to possess strong appetites for power, because with extraordinary power comes extraordinary reproduction." As evidence, he notes that many ancient warrior-kings kept harems of hundreds of fertile females.

The Absence of the War Gene

But significantly, most authorities on the origins of warfare reject the fatalistic notion that war is an inevitable consequence of our biology. The anthropologist Jonathan Haas, of the University of Illinois at Chicago, points out that rates of warfare have always fluctuated both between and within societies, contradicting the "preposterous" notion that warfare is so innate that it is inevitable. "If war is deeply rooted in our biology, then it's going to be there all the time," he says. "And it's just not." War, he argues, is certainly not innate in the same sense as language, which has been exhibited by all known human societies at all times.

The anthropologists Carol and Melvin Ember agree that biological theories cannot explain patterns of warfare among either pre-state or state societies. The Embers oversee Yale University's Human Relations Area Files, a database of information on some 360 cultures past and present. More than 90 percent of those societies have engaged in warfare, but some have fought constantly and others rarely, while a few have never been observed fighting. The Embers have found correlations between rates of warfare and environmental factors, notably droughts, floods, and other natural disasters that provoke fears of famine.

Even scientists whose work seems to support fatalism toward war dismiss that attitude themselves. One is the anthropologist Napoleon Chagnon, of the University of California at Santa Barbara, who is renowned for finding a link between male violence and reproductive success among the Yanomamo, a warlike tribal society in the Amazon that he has studied since the 1960s. According to Chagnon, Yanomamo killers have, on average, twice as many wives and three times as many children as male nonkillers in the tribe.

But Chagnon has always denied that Yanomamo men fight because of a "war gene" or instinct. Truly compulsive, out-of-control killers, he notes, are quickly killed themselves. Successful warriors are usually quite calculating, he says; they fight because that is how a man advances in their society. Moreover, many Yanomamo men have confessed to Chagnon that they loathe war and wish it could be abolished from their culture—and, in fact, rates of violence have recently dropped sharply, as Yanomamo villages have accepted the laws and mores of the outside world.

Pacifying Warlike Cultures

History offers many other examples of warlike societies that rapidly became peaceful. Vikings were the scourge of Europe during the Middle Ages, but their Scandinavian descendants are among the most peaceful people on earth. Similarly, Germany and Japan, which just 70 years ago were the world's most militaristic, aggressive nations, have embraced pacifism, albeit after catastrophic defeats.

Primate studies also offer grounds for optimism. The primatologist Frans de Waal, of Emory University, has demonstrated that shifts in environmental conditions can reduce primate violence. In one of his experiments, rhesus monkeys, which are ordinarily incorrigibly aggressive, grew up to become kinder and gentler when raised by mild-mannered stumptail monkeys. De Waal has reduced conflicts among monkeys and apes by increasing their interdependence—making them cooperate to obtain food, for example—and ensuring their equal access to food.

He has also drawn attention to the remarkable chimpanzee species Pan paniscus. More commonly known as bonobos, they are darker-skinned and slimmer than chimpanzees and have markedly different lifestyles. "No deadly warfare," de Waal comments, "little hunting, no male dominance, and enormous amounts of sex." That promiscuity, he speculates, reduces violence both within and between bonobo troops, just as intermarriage does between human tribes.

The Stanford biologist Robert Sapolsky points out that environmental conditions can override biology even among baboons, which are ordinarily extremely aggressive. Since the early 1980s, Sapolsky has traveled to Kenya to spy on what he calls the Forest Troop, a group of baboons living near a garbage dump. Because they had to fight baboons from another troop camped nearby, only the toughest males of Forest Troop frequented the dump. In the mid-1980s, all those males died after contracting tuberculosis from contaminated meat at the dump.

The epidemic left Forest Troop with many more females than males, and with noticeably less-pugnacious males. Conflict within the troop plummeted; Sapolsky even observed males grooming one another, which he says is "nearly as un-precedented as baboons sprouting wings." This sea change has persisted. "Is a world of peacefully coexisting human Forest Troops possible?" Sapolsky asks. "Anyone who says, 'No, it is beyond our nature,' knows too little about primates, including ourselves."

The World Is More Peaceful Nowadays

The message that I hammer home in class is that—contrary to the impression created by news headlines—humanity as a whole is much less warlike than it used to be. In other words: Things are getting better! World Wars I and II and all the other horrific conflicts of the 20th century resulted in the deaths of fewer than 3 percent of the global population. According to Lawrence Keeley, that is an order of magnitude less than the rate of violent death for men in the average primitive society, whose weapons consisted only of clubs and spears rather than machine guns and bombs.

If war is defined as an armed conflict leading to at least 1,000 deaths per year, there have been relatively few international wars since World War II, and civil wars have declined sharply since peaking in the early 1990s. Most conflicts now consist of guerrilla wars, insurgencies, and terrorism—or what the political scientist John Mueller, of Ohio State University, calls the "remnants of war." He rejects biological explanations for the trend, noting that "testosterone levels seem to be as high as ever." While acknowledging that many political scientists still consider war to be "an inevitable part of international and domestic life," Mueller asserts that "a continuing decline in war does seem to be an entirely reasonable prospect."

The cognitive psychologist Steven Pinker identifies several possible reasons for the recent decline of violence. First, the creation of stable states with effective legal systems and police forces has eliminated the Hobbesian [after the theories of English philosopher Thomas Hobbes] anarchy of all against all. Second, our increased life expectancies make us less willing to risk our lives by engaging in violence. Third, as a result of globalization and communications, we have become increasingly interdependent on, and empathetic toward, others outside of our immediate tribes.

In short, many lines of research contradict the myth that war is a constant of the human condition. Those studies also suggest that—contrary to the myth of the peaceful, noble savage—civilization has not created the problem of warfare; it is helping us solve it. We need more civilization, not less, if we wish to eradicate war. Civilization has given us legal institutions that resolve disputes by establishing laws, negotiating agreements, and enforcing them. Those institutions, which range from local courts to the United Nations, have vastly reduced the risk of violence both within and between nations.

Possible Solutions to Warfare

Obviously, our institutions are far from perfect. Nations around the world still maintain huge arsenals, including weapons of mass destruction, and armed conflicts still ravage many regions. So what should we do? The anthropologist and psychiatrist Melvin Konner proposes female education as one key to reducing conflict. Many studies, he notes, have demonstrated that an increase in the education of women leads to a decrease in birth rates. The result is a stabilized population, which decreases demands on governmental and medical services and on natural resources, and hence decreases the likelihood of social unrest. A lower birth rate also reduces what some demographers call "bare branches": unmarried, unemployed young men, who are associated with higher rates of violent conflict both within and between nations. "Education of girls is by far the best investment you can make in a developing country," Konner says.

In my course, we discuss many other possible solutions to warfare, such as decreasing severe poverty and ensuring a more equitable distribution of food, water, and other resources; developing cheap, clean, renewable sources of energy; creating a global government with the power to anticipate and quell outbreaks of violence; and promoting the spread of participatory democracy. Chances are that none of those solutions will be sufficient in and of itself. War seems to be overdetermined, springing from many different causes, not all of which are necessary for war to occur. Peace, if it is to last, must be overdetermined, too.

My overarching goal in "War and Human Nature" is to persuade my scientifically oriented students to see war not as a permanent part of the human condition, stemming from our genes or original sin, but as a potentially solvable scientific problem. To be sure, war is a dauntingly complex phenomenon, with political, economic, and social ramifications. But the same could be said of problems such as global warming, overpopulation, and AIDS, all of which are being rigorously addressed by scientists.

Peace is a challenge at least as worthy of pursuit as cheap, clean, renewable sources of energy or cures for AIDS or cancer. War research would be the ultimate multidisciplinary enterprise, drawing upon such diverse fields as game theory, neurobiology, evolutionary psychology, theology, ecology, political science, and economics. The short-term goal of researchers would be to find ways to reduce conflict in the world, wherever it might occur. The long-term goal would be to explore how nations can make the transition toward eliminating or at least greatly reducing armies and arsenals, including weapons of mass destruction.

In a famous 1906 essay, [American psychologist and philosopher] William James acknowledged that war fulfills deep human, especially male, needs. "The plain truth is that people want war," he wrote. We can eradicate war, he contended, only by finding a substitute, "the moral equivalent of war," to challenge and engage young men. James proposed enlisting them in a "war against nature," engaging in perilous occupations such as mining, logging, and fishing. I have a better idea: Make peace the moral equivalent of war for all young people.

Soldiers Have a Difficult Time Adjusting to Life After War

Brian Mockenhaupt

Brian Mockenhaupt is a former U.S. Marine who served in Iraq. He is now a contributing editor to Esquire *magazine.*

In the following viewpoint, Mockenhaupt draws on his own experiences in claiming that soldiers who return home from combat often miss the excitement and tension of their tours of duty. Holding a weapon and being involved in battle is an adrenaline rush that changes the way soldiers see life, Mockenhaupt attests. When that element is removed, he claims, they crave the experience because it is more intense, more vivid, and more fun than the normal day-to-day responsibilities that make up average lives. Mockenhaupt goes further, insisting that soldiers are not the only ones seduced by the power of warfare; most people, in his view, are fascinated by war even if they recognize the death and destruction it entails.

A few months ago, I found a Web site loaded with pictures and videos from Iraq, the sort that usually aren't seen on the news. I watched insurgent snipers shoot American soldiers and car bombs disintegrate markets, accompanied by tinny music and loud, rhythmic chanting, the soundtrack of the propaganda campaigns. Video cameras focused on empty stretches of road, building anticipation. Humvees rolled into view and the explosions brought mushroom clouds of dirt and smoke and chunks of metal spinning through the air. Other videos and pictures showed insurgents shot dead while planting roadside bombs or killed in firefights and the remains of suicide bombers, people how they're not meant to be seen, no longer whole. The images sickened me, but their familiarity pulled me in, giving comfort, and I couldn't stop. I clicked through more frames, hungry for it. This must be what a shot of dope feels like after a long stretch of sobriety. Soothing and nauseating and colored by everything that has come before. My body tingled and my stomach ached, hollow. I stood on weak legs and walked into the kitchen to make dinner. I sliced half an onion before putting the knife down and watching slight tremors run through my hand. The shakiness lingered. I drank a beer. And as I leaned against this kitchen counter, in this house, in America, my life felt very foreign.

Missing the War

I've been home from Iraq for more than a year, long enough for my time there to become a memory best forgotten for those who worried every day that I was gone. I could see their relief when I returned. Life could continue, with futures not so uncertain. But in quiet moments, their relief brought me guilt. Maybe they assume I was as overjoyed to be home as they were to have me home. Maybe they assume if I could do it over, I never would have gone. And maybe I wouldn't have. But I miss Iraq. I miss the war. I miss war. And I have a very hard time understanding why.

I'm glad to be home, to have put away my uniforms, to wake up next to my wife each morning. I worry about my friends who are in Iraq now, and I wish they weren't. Often I hated being there, when the frustrations and lack of control over my life were complete and mind-bending. I questioned my role in the occupation and whether good could come of it. I wondered if it was worth dying or killing for. The suffering and ugliness I saw disgusted me. But war twists and shifts the landmarks by which we navigate our lives, casting light on darkened areas that for many people remain forever unexplored. And once those darkened spaces are lit, they become part of us. At a party several years ago, long before the Army, I listened to a friend who had served several years in the Marines tell a woman that if she carried a pistol for a day, just tucked in her waistband and out of sight, she would feel different. She would see the world differently, for better or worse. Guns empower. She disagreed and he shrugged. No use arguing the point; he was just offering a little piece of truth. He was right, of course. And that's just the beginning.

I've spent hours taking in the world through a rifle scope, watching life unfold. Women hanging laundry on a rooftop. Men haggling over a hindquarter of lamb in the market. Children walking to school. I've watched this and hoped that someday I would see that my presence had made their lives better, a redemption of sorts. But I also peered through the scope waiting for someone to do something wrong, so I could shoot him. When you pick up a weapon with the intent of killing, you step onto a very strange and serious playing field. Every morning someone wakes wanting to kill you. When you walk down the street, they are waiting, and you want to kill them, too. That's not bloodthirsty; that's just the trade you've learned. And as an American soldier, you have a very impressive toolbox. You can fire your rifle or lob a grenade, and if that's not enough, call in the tanks, or helicopters, or jets. The insurgents have their skill sets, too, turning mornings at the market into chaos, crowds into scattered flesh, Humvees into charred scrap. You're all part of the terrible magic show, both powerful and helpless.

An Exciting, Intense Experience

That men are drawn to war is no surprise. How old are boys before they turn a finger and thumb into a pistol? Long before they love girls, they love war, at least everything they imagine war to be: guns and explosions and manliness and courage. When my neighbors and I played war as kids, there was no fear or sorrow or cowardice. Death was temporary, usually as fast as you could count to sixty and jump back into the game. We didn't know yet about the darkness. And young men are just slightly older versions of those boys, still loving the unknown, perhaps pumped up on dreams of duty and heroism and the intoxicating power of weapons. In time, war dispels many such notions, and more than a few men find that being freed from society's professed revulsion to killing is really no freedom at all, but a lonely burden. Yet even at its lowest points, war is like nothing else. Our culture craves experience, and that is war's strong suit. War peels back the skin, and you live with a layer of nerves exposed, overdosing on your surroundings, when everything seems all wrong and just right, in a way that makes perfect sense. And then you almost die but don't, and are born again, stoned on life and mocking death. The explosions and gunfire fry your nerves, but you want to hear them all the same. Something's going down.

For those who know, this is the open secret: War is exciting. Sometimes I was in awe of this, and sometimes I felt low and mean for loving it, but I loved it still. Even in its quiet moments, war is brighter, louder, brasher, more fun, more tragic, more wasteful. More. More of everything. And even then I knew I would someday miss it, this life so strange. Today the war has distilled to moments and feelings, and somewhere in these memories is the reason for the wistfulness. . . .

After watching the Internet videos, I called some of my friends who are out of the Army now, and they miss the war, too. Wells very nearly died in Iraq. A sniper shot him in the head, surgeons cut out half of his skull and he spent months in therapy, working back to his old self. Now he misses the high. "I don't want to sound like a psychopath, but you're like a god over there," he says. "It might not be the best kind of adrenaline for you, but it's a rush." Before Iraq, he didn't care for horror movies, and now he's drawn to them. He watches them for the little thrill, the rush of being startled, if just for a moment. . . .

Mortal danger heightens the senses. That is simple animal instinct. We're more aware of how our world smells and sounds and tastes. This distorts and enriches experiences. Now I can have everything, but it's not as good as when I could have none of it. McCarthy and I stood on a rooftop one afternoon in Iraq running through a long list of the food we wanted. We made it to homemade pizza and icy beer when someone loosed a long burst of gunfire that cracked over our heads. We ran to the other side of the rooftop, but the gunman had disappeared down a long alleyway. Today my memory of that pizza and beer is stronger than if McCarthy and I had sat down together with the real thing before us.

And today we even speak with affection of wrestling a dead man into a body bag, because that was then. The bullet had laid his thigh wide open, shattered the femur, and shredded the artery, so he'd bled out fast, pumping much of his blood onto the sidewalk. We unfolded and unzipped the nylon sack and laid it alongside him. And then we stared for a moment, none of us ready to close that distance. I grabbed his forearm and dropped it, maybe instinct, maybe revulsion. He hovered so near this world, having just passed over, that he seemed to be sucking life from me, pulling himself back or taking me with him. He peeked at us through a half-opened eye. I stared down on him, his massive dead body, and again wrapped a hand around his wrist, thick and warm. The man was huge, taller than six feet and close to 250 pounds. We strained with the awkward weight, rolled him into the bag, and zipped him out of sight. My platoon sergeant gave two neighborhood kids five dollars to wash away the congealing puddle of blood. But the red handprint stayed on the wall, where the man had tried to brace himself before he fell. I think about him sometimes, splayed out on the sidewalk, and I think of how lucky I was never to have put a friend in one of those bags. Or be put in one myself.

U.S. Army Pfc. Wayne Gonzalez and his eight-month-old daughter. In this viewpoint Brian Mockenhaupt argues that soldiers often have difficulty adjusting to civilian life because it lacks the intensity of war. Chris Hondros/Getty Images.

Everyone Wants a Bit of Darkness

But the memories, good and bad, are only part of the reason war holds its grip long after soldiers have come home. The war was urgent and intense and the biggest story going, always on the news stations and magazine covers. At home, though, relearning everyday life, the sense of mission can be hard to find. And this is not just about dim prospects and low-paying jobs in small towns. Leaving the war behind can be a letdown, regardless of opportunity or education or the luxuries waiting at home. People I'd never met sent me boxes of cookies and candy throughout my tours. When I left for two weeks of leave, I was cheered at airports and hugged by strangers. At dinner with my family one night, a man from the next table bought me a $400 bottle of wine. I was never quite comfortable with any of this, but they were heady moments nonetheless. For my friends who are going back to Iraq or are there already, there is little enthusiasm. Any fondness for war is tainted by the practicalities of operating and surviving in combat. Wells and McCarthy and I can speak of the war with nostalgia because we belong to a different world now. And yet there is little to say, because we are scattered, far from those who understand. . . .

When I came home, people often asked me about Iraq, and mostly I told them it wasn't so bad. The first few times, my wife asked me why I had been so blithe. Why didn't I tell them what Iraq was really like? I don't know how to explain myself to them. The war wasn't really so bad. Yes, there were bombs and shootings and nervous times, but that was just the job. In fact, going to war is rather easy. You react to situations around you and try not to die. There are no electric bills or car payments or chores around the house. Just go to work, come home alive, and do it again tomorrow. McCarthy calls it pure and serene. Indeed. Life at home can be much more trying. But I didn't imagine the people asking would understand that. I didn't care much if they did, and often it seemed they just wanted a war story, a bit of grit and gore. If they really want to know, thay can always find out for themselves. But they don't, they just want a taste of the thrill. We all do. We covet life outside our bubble. That's why we love tragedy, why we love hearing about war and death on the television, drawn to it in spite of ourselves. We gawk at accident scenes and watch people humiliate themselves on reality shows and can't wait to replay the events for friends, as though in retelling the story we make it our own, if just for the moment.

We live easy third-person lives but want a bit of the darkness. War fascinates because we live so far from its realities. Maybe we'd feel differently about watching bombs blow up on TV if we saw them up close, if we knew how explosions rip the air, throttle your brain, and make your ears ring, if we knew the strain of wondering whether the car next to you at a traffic light would explode or a bomb would land on your house as you sleep. I don't expect Iraqi soldiers would ever miss war. I have that luxury. I came home to peace, to a country that hasn't seen war within its borders for nearly 150 years. Yes, some boys come home dead. But we live here without the other terrors and tragedies of war—cities flattened and riven with chaos and fear, neighbors killing one another, a people made forever weary by the violence.

And so I miss it. . . .

Robot Soldiers Can Create a More Ethical Battlefield

Ronald C. Arkin

Ronald C. Arkin is a professor at the Georgia Institute of Technology, where he is also director of the Mobile Robot Laboratory.

In The Red Badge of Courage, *emotions drove Henry Fleming to cowardice and bravery on the battlefield. In the combat zone of the future, robots could be employed to rid the battlefield of such emotions. In the viewpoint that follows, Arkin argues that robotic soldiers can be programmed to pursue their mission without the influence of passions such as rage and revenge. In this respect, Arkin claims that robots might fight more ethically than humans do. In his opinion, robots could be programmed to adhere to a set of laws governing warfare, making them fight only in sanctioned ways. This would reduce human, noncombatant casualties and the occurrence of war crimes in tomorrow's conflicts, Arkin concludes.*

Robotic system capabilities have advanced dramatically over the last several decades. We now have artificially intelligent systems and robots that are stronger than humans, that can venture places where people cannot go (such as Mars), that are smarter than people in certain cases (e.g., in chess), and so on. We are no longer truly surprised when machine artifacts outperform humans in new domains. But the outperformance of humans by artificially intelligent systems may still come as a surprise to some. It is a thesis of my ongoing research for the U.S. Army that robots not only can be better than soldiers in conducting warfare in certain circumstances, but they also can be more humane in the battlefield than humans.

Ronald C. Arkin, "Ethical Robots in Warfare," *IEEE Technology & Society Magazine*, vol. 28, no. 1, Spring 2009, pp. 30–33. Copyright © 2009 IEEE. Reproduced by permission.

Toward Robotic Autonomy

Why should this surprise us? Do we believe that human soldiers exhibit the best of humanity in battlefield situations? There is strong evidence to the contrary and we have developed Laws of War to criminalize those people who behave outside of acceptable international norms. Despite these regulations, they are often cast aside in the heat of combat, for reasons such as vengeance, anger, frustration, and the desire for victory at any cost.

Robots already have the ability to carry weapons and to use lethal force under the direction of a human operator. Multiple unmanned robotic systems are already being developed or are in use that employ lethal force such as the Armed Robotic Vehicle (ARV), a component of the Future Combat System (FCS); Predator and Reaper unmanned aerial vehicles (UAVs) equipped with hellfire missiles, which have already been used in combat but under direct human supervision; and the development of an armed platform for use in the Korean Demilitarized Zone, to name only a few. These and other systems are not fully autonomous in this sense: they do not currently make decisions on their own about when, or whether or not, to engage a target. But the pressure of an increasing battlefield tempo is forcing autonomy further and further towards the point of robots making that final, lethal decision. The time available to make the decision to shoot or not to shoot is becoming too short for remote humans to make intelligent, informed decisions in many situations that arise in modern warfare. As that time dwindles, robots will likely be given more authority to make lethal decisions on their own.

Commercially available robots already have had "emotions" engineered into them, e.g., the robot dog AIBO. Researchers, at least to some extent, have an understanding of what affect contributes to intelligent interaction with humans. It is my contention that robots can be built that do not exhibit fear, anger, frustration, or revenge, and that ultimately (and the key word here is ultimately) behave in a more humane manner than even human beings in these harsh circumstances and severe duress. People have not evolved to function in these conditions, but robots can be engineered to function well in them.

Robot Adherence to Laws of War

In a forthcoming book entitled *Governing Lethal Behavior in Autonomous Robots*, I make the case that autonomous armed robotic platforms may ultimately reduce noncombatant casualties and other forms of collateral damage by their ability to better adhere to the Laws of War than most soldiers possibly can. Some of the material that follows is drawn directly from this book. Many of my colleagues ... argue against this thesis and bring up many significant issues that must be resolved prior to such a deployment. To summarize both sides of these arguments, first, the reasons why ethical autonomy can succeed include the following.

- The ability to act conservatively: Robots do not need to protect themselves in cases of low certainty of target identification. Autonomous armed robotic vehicles do not need to have self-preservation as a foremost drive, if at all. They can be used in a self-sacrificing manner if needed and appropriate, without reservation by a commanding officer.

- The eventual development and use of a broad range of robotic sensors better equipped for battlefield observations than human sensory abilities.

- Robots can be designed without emotions that cloud their judgment or result in anger and frustration with ongoing battlefield events. In addition, "Fear and hysteria are always latent in combat, often real, and they press us toward fearful measures and criminal behavior". Autonomous agents need not suffer similarly.

- Avoidance of the human psychological problem of "scenario fulfillment" is possible, a factor believed partly contributing to the downing of an Iranian airliner by the USS Vincennes in 1988. This phenomenon leads to distortion or neglect of contradictory information in stressful situations, where humans use new incoming information in ways that fit only their pre-existing belief patterns, a form of premature cognitive closure. Robots need not be vulnerable to such patterns of behavior.

- Before responding with lethal forces, robots can integrate more information from more sources far more quickly than a human can in real time. This information and data can arise from multiple remote sensors and intelligence (including human) sources, as part of the Army's network-centric warfare concept and the concurrent development of the Global Information Grid. "Military systems (including weapons) now on the horizon will be too fast, too small, too numerous, and will create an environment too complex for humans to direct".

- When working on a team of combined human soldiers and autonomous systems as an organic asset, robots have the potential to independently and objectively monitor ethical behavior in the battlefield by all parties and report infractions that might be observed. This presence alone might possibly lead to a reduction in human ethical infractions.

Additional Benefits

Aside from these ethical considerations, autonomous robotic systems offer numerous potential operational benefits to the military: faster, cheaper, better mission accomplishment; longer range, greater persistence, longer endurance, higher precision; faster target engagement; and immunity to chemical and biological weapons. All of these can enhance mission effectiveness and serve as drivers for the ongoing deployment of these systems.

But this new research focuses on enhancing ethical benefits by using these systems, ideally without eroding mission performance when compared to human fighters.

Arguments Against Robots

The counterarguments against the use of lethal autonomous systems are numerous as well:

- Establishing responsibility—who's to blame if things go wrong with an autonomous robot?
- The threshold of entry into warfare may be lowered as we will now be risking machines and fewer human soldiers—this could violate the Jus ad Bellum [literally, "law/right to war"] conditions of just warfare.
- The possibility of unilateral risk-free warfare, which could be viewed as potentially unjust.
- It simply can't be done right—it's just too hard for machines to discriminate targets.
- The effect on military squad cohesion and its impact on the fighting force—human fighters may not accept ethical robots monitoring their performance.
- Robots running amok—the classic science fiction nightmare.
- A robot refusing an order—the question of whether ultimate authority should vest in humans.
- The issues of overrides placed in the hands of immoral, irresponsible, or reckless individuals.
- The co-opting of an ethical robot research effort by the military to serve to justify other political agendas.

- The difficulty in winning the hearts and minds of the civilians affected by warfare if robots are allowed to kill.

- Proliferation of the technology to other nations and terrorists.

I am confident these contrarian issues are raised in more detail [elsewhere] and I will not elaborate on them here. Some are more easily dismissed than others. Some are not unique to autonomous robot battlefield technology. Some can be addressed by recognizing that we're dealing with bounded morality for very narrow tactical situations and are not replacing a human soldier one-for-one. And some can be addressed by suitable system design which may be long range but nonetheless feasible. Space, however, prevents a full and fair treatment of these concerns here.

The goal of my research on ethical autonomous systems capable of lethal action is to provide robots with an ethical code that has been already established by humanity as encoded in the Laws of War and the Rules of Engagement. Robots must be constrained to adhere to the same laws as humans or they should not be permitted on the battlefield. This further implies that they must have the right to refuse an order which is determined to be unethical, and that they possess the ability to monitor and report on the ethical behavior of other military personnel as required.

Ethical Responsibilities

I think of myself as a responsible scientist who has spent decades working on military applications of robotics. I think the following questions are crucial:

Is it not our responsibility as scientists to look for effective ways to reduce human inhumanity to other people through technology? And if such inhumanity occurs during warfare, what can be done?

It is my belief that research in ethical military robotics can and should be applied towards achieving this end. But how can this happen? Where does humanity fit on the battlefield? Extrapolating these questions further, we ask:

Should soldiers be robots?

Isn't that largely what they are trained to be?

Should robots be soldiers?

Could they be more humane than humans?

One lesson I have learned along the way is that roboticists should not run from the difficult ethical issues surrounding the use of their intellectual property that is or will be applied to warfare, whether or not they directly participate. Wars unfortunately will continue and derivative technology from these ideas will be used. If your robotics research is of significance and it is published openly, it will be put to use in military systems by someone, somewhere, someday. Researchers are not immune from contributing to military applications by simply not accepting funds from the U.S. Department of Defense (DoD). To ensure proper usage of this technology, proactive management by all parties concerned is necessary. . . .

I remain active in my research for the U.S. DoD in battlefield applications of robotics for both the U.S. Army and Navy regarding the deployment of teams of robots, but it remains a personal goal that these systems and other related military research products will ultimately be ethically restrained by technological methods . . . so as to abide by the internationally agreed upon Laws of War. I also hope that this research will spur others into not only considering this problem, but to help ensure that warfare is conducted justly, even with the advent of autonomous robots if international societies so deem it fit, and that those who step beyond those ethical bounds, whoever they may be, are successfully prosecuted for their war crimes. It is my conviction that as these weaponized autonomous systems appear on the battlefield, they should help to ensure that humanity, proportionality, responsibility, and relative safety, as encoded in the Laws of War, are extended during combat not only to friendly forces, but equally to non-combatants and those who are otherwise hors de combat [outside of combat]. The goal will be a reduction in the loss of life of civilians and all other forms of collateral damage.

Changes in America's Armed Forces Make War a Less Costly Decision

Jason Royce Lindsey

Jason Royce Lindsey is an associate professor of political science at St. Cloud State University in Minnesota.

In the following viewpoint, Lindsey states that today the United States is able to use military force almost at will because the Department of Defense is making it less costly for America to engage in warfare. In Lindsey's view, advances in technology and medicine have reduced battlefield casualties, and the replacement of soldiers with robots, animals, and contracted mercenaries has eliminated some of the ethical charges leveled at the continual deployment of troops into harm's way. Removing such points of contention from the debate over the use of military force has weakened political and civil opposition to deployment, Lindsey claims, and subsequently bolstered America's tolerance for war.

The importance of domestic political pressure as a restraint on America's use of force has become more apparent with the current conflict in Iraq. In our post–Cold War international environment, there is no large rival to inhibit U.S. action. Current international organizations are unable to serve as a substitute source of pressure. Thus, while the United States is without an equal international rival, only American citizens can provide an effective political check to their government's use of force. Many Americans, however, seem remarkably apathetic. This irony is due to recent developments in the structure and technology of the American mili-

Jason Royce Lindsey, "America and the New Dynamics of War," *Peace Review: A Journal of Social Justice*, vol. 19, no. 2, April–June 2007, pp. 255–260. Copyright © 2007 Taylor & Francis Group, LLC. Reproduced by permission of Taylor & Francis, Ltd., http//:www.tandf.co.uk/journals and the author.

tary establishment. What is emerging is a military structure that the United States can deploy with less domestic political cost to the American government. The consequences of this change are profound for the United States and the world.

One of the key trends within this troubling change is the increasing compartmentalization of the military from the rest of American society. Many observers, especially abroad, are puzzled by the small amount of political protest in the United States over the war in Iraq. What this point of view fails to see are the changes that have occurred within the U.S. armed forces and American society since the 1970s. The critical difference is that, unlike the past, today's military practically constitutes a separate social class within American society. As an all-volunteer body, with many life-long members, deployment of this professional military force does not create domestic political opposition like the 1960s conscript army that was sent to Vietnam.

Instead, the modern American military relies on a core of full-time military personnel who have chosen the service as a career. Many Americans choose the military career path in an effort to move up in society from poorer backgrounds. Studies of military recruitment consistently show that the service's most significant appeal to young people is its educational benefits. Individuals enlisting in the military after high school earn college tuition credits for each year they serve. Although feelings of patriotism are also important to military recruitment, studies consistently show that the military's chief attraction is the social mobility it brings. Surveys show, for example, that high school students with college eductaed parents and higher grades in school are less likely to enlist. In addition, traditionally poorer ethnic minorities, specifically African Americans and Hispanics, are more likely to enlist than their white peers are. Thus, military service often provides a path to college and social advancement for individuals with less affluent origins in Ameican society.

Although this professional volunteer force is ethnically and regionally diverse, it remains concentrated in specific, cohesive communities. This slice of the American population lives on or near military installations across the United States, and learns to expect deployment as a possibility. Divisions within this community do exist, such as that between higher-level officers from the prestigious American military academies and lower-ranking soldiers. The neighborhoods near military bases across the United States, however, are some of the most racially integrated in the country. This social cohesion sets these communities apart from others across the United States. In surveys of opinion, military personnel drawn from similar backgrounds in American society and with similar career paths show significant attitudinal differences from civilians. From this perspective, U.S. military personnel live in tight-knit communities that are supportive of soldiers and families, but are also disconnected from the average American's daily life.

On this point, it is noticeable that the major source of resentment toward the current war is from the National Guard and Reserve members' families. These reservists traditionally support full-time soldiers as needed during emergencies. The Iraq conflict, however, has seen many National Guard units deployed for 12 or more months at a time, depending on the unit and its specialization. This group is drawn from a much more inclusive cross-section of the citizenry compared to the compartmentalized career soldiers. As a result, deployment of the National Guard has been one of the more politically difficult aspects of the war for the current administration.

Further deployments of reserve units would be necessary if the professional army were not also supported by so-called contract soldiers serving with U.S. forces in Iraq. Contract soldiers are employees of private American companies under contract with the U.S. Department of Defense. Currently, these contract soldiers are one of the largest contingents of coalition troops in Iraq and are almost equal in size to the

British contribution. These mercenary forces perform a broad range of functions that used to be the exclusive responsibility of U.S. troops. The most elastic of these duties, security, allows contract soldiers to fill critical gaps in the overstretched volunteer army. Given this group's monetary motive for being in Iraq, it is not plausible to expect any political pressure from the public over casualties in this group. Indeed, the casualties from the contract forces are largely invisible because the media does not give them the same attention as other battlefield deaths. So far, the only controversy surrounding these mercenary troops has been the implication of some "contractors" in the questionable interrogation techniques used at Abu Ghraib.

Besides these structural changes to the military's composition, improvements in weaponry and battlefield medicine have held American casualties in Iraq to a minimum. Compared to the Vietnam conflict, fewer American soldiers die on the battlefield or are permanently incapacitated. Improvements that cost the United States less lives on the battlefield make the overall likelihood of using force more likely. This tragic paradox stems from the simple political calculation that force is easier to apply the lower its cost in American lives. Thus, fewer casualties increase the likelihood of some lives being lost because all deployments are politically cheaper.

The decline in American military deaths through better battlefield medicine also corresponds to an increased effectiveness on the battlefield. With improvements in military weaponry and technology, fewer soldiers can cover larger areas of occupation. Thus, American military forces can occupy a country the size of Iraq, at least tenuously, with a relatively small force of about 160,000 troops. The result of these two trends is fewer forces deployed and fewer casualties from that smaller force.

Another irony of this situation is that improvements in battlefield medicine and weapons technology that save the life of the common American soldier also increase the odds of

Joint Direct Attack Munitions (JDAMs), guidance kits that convert unguided bombs into precision-guided "smart" munitions, are loaded aboard the USS Truman. *The author contends that technology that allows troops to stay out of harm's way reduces ethical concerns about collateral damage and raises people's tolerance for entering into war.* Danny Ewing Jr./U.S. Navy/Getty Images.

collateral damage affecting foreign civilians. For example, reliance on cruise missiles and air strikes reduces American military deaths, but this is offset by the likelihood of injuring innocent bystanders. Estimates of Iraqi civilian deaths range in the tens of thousands. Yet, large numbers of Iraqi civilian deaths have so far failed to make a strong impression on the American public. The moral logic of distinguishing between the two groups is tragically nearsighted. Even by conservative estimates, the total number of Iraqi civilian deaths since the American-led invasion began is far beyond the number of U.S. military casualties. Besides the immediate suffering these deaths represent for the people of Iraq, this violence has triggered an exodus of the country's middle class and best educated. Thus, Iraq will continue to feel the consequences of this population loss for decades to come.

Nonetheless, American politicians know that American military casualties are significant in domestic politics, not the innocents caught in the fray a world away from their constituents. So, as the political costs for using military force come down through fewer battlefield deaths and the deployment of smaller, compartmentalized forces, it is easier for this and future American administrations to use force.

Further technological developments are likely to continue this political trend. Recent reports in the news media and scholarly sources, for example, reveal that the U.S. Department of Defense is investing heavily in robotics research. This priority is supported by an enthusiastic U.S. Congress that has consistently increased funding in this area over the last few years. The military already uses robots to help with bomb disposal and other dangerous tasks. Most impressive to date has been the increased use of robotic aircraft, drones, for aerial reconnaissance and remotely controlled air strikes.

Besides robotics, reports of even more bizarre military research, with far-reaching ethical consequences and questions, have appeared in the American and British media. The research arm of the Department of Defense, DARPA, has been experimenting with the remote control of animals. Apparently, one of their largest experiments has involved using sharks for naval reconnaissance. The sharks have electronics implanted in them allowing an operator to steer them toward a chosen target. DARPA has pioneered this line of research because using a living organism, like a shark, saves much time and cost over developing a machine to do the same task (that is, to swim like a shark). The research is attempting to ascertain the feasibility of using sharks and other modified animals for dangerous reconaissance missions.

The instrumental logic driving these developments in technology and capability raise a fundamental question for a democratic state. If robots, machines, and modified animals make up an increasingly significant element of United States fighting forces, then what will happen to the politics of military action?

One obvious point is that the use of machines and other substitutes for human soldiers reduces the political pressure on policymakers. The public's tolerance for casualties is an important calculation when a democracy goes to war. With the increased use of machines, this political pressure can be reduced in future wars. Therefore, current trends within the American military establishment may make it much easier for politicians to support future wars. This possibility represents a challenge to long-held assumptions about democracies and war.

In political philosophy, theorists have long assumed that one of the responsibilities of democratic citizens is defense of the state. Modern political scientists, who have been concerned with the public's lack of interest in foreign policy, knew that voters would at least pay attention on issues of war and peace. This traditional assumption is often cited as an important advantage of democracy. Many argue that democratic governments are more pacific since citizen armies will only support wars that are vital for self-defense. Yet, this traditional assumption, already debatable, is made even less plausible by career, volunteer armies and technologies that replace human soldiers.

Therefore, all of us face a future where the responsibility of defense and the cost of war will be shifted to machines and become a more technocratic area of policy. Although this may sound farfetched, a straightforward logic drives the U.S. Department of Defense. We see today that the use of a compartmentalized volunteer force, military contractors, and new technologies is reducing the political costs of war in Iraq. This same line of reasoning, when connected with future robotic technology, will transform the issue of war and its costs even more dramatically in the years to come.

This shift in how wars are fought will exacerbate the gap in power that exists in the world. It is easy to imagine a future where developed, wealthy countries can easily threaten military action by risking machines rather than citizens in combat. On the other side, poorer, less developed states would be faced with the less credible threat of putting their citizens on the line to face military machines. In such a scenario, it is easy to see that the power gap between developed and underdeveloped states will only widen in years to come.

How will poorer and developing states react to this dynamic? We already see one strategy in the actions of Iran and North Korea. If poorer states cannot hope to compete with the United States and other developed countries by conventional means, then the logical move is to look for a cheap equalizer: nuclear and ballistic missile programs. In the future, if one cannot hope to match a state-of-the-art military like that of the United States on the battlefield, then the only logical deterrent are weapons that threaten its homeland citizens.

What should be the reaction of citizens in the United States and its allies to these trends? As the military power of the United States and other developed countries accelerates, the moral responsibility for using it will shift more and more to the citizenry. In a sense, this moral obligation is increasing proportionally to the ease with which government officials can apply force. As future policymakers face fewer traditional restraints on the use of military force, the burden for filling this gap with new domestic political pressure rests with the citizenry. This same dynamic will spread to other developed countries that can emulate the structure and technology of America's military.

Thus, the fate of a shrinking group of domestic professional soldiers and a growing throng of civilians everywhere depends on the action of citizens in the United States and other developed countries. To address this emerging dynamic, urgent debate is needed on the broad but interrelated topics discussed here. If citizens engage their political leaders on this issue, then perhaps the old assumption about democracies being averse to war will continue. Otherwise, this next century will see the wealthiest and most powerful states, in the absence of domestic political pressure, free to use force as never before.

Recommended Readings

Adams, Thomas K. 2001–2002. "Future Warfare and the Decline of Human Decision Making," *Parameters* 31 (Winter): 51–71.

Bekey, George A. 2005. *Autonomous Robots: From Biological Inspiration to Implementation and Control.* Cambridge, MA: MIT Press.

Brown, Susan. 2006. "Stealth Sharks to Patrol the High Seas." *The New Scientist.* 2541, March 1:30.

Eighmey, John. 2006. "Why Do Youth Enlist: Identification of Underlying Themes," *Armed Forces and Society* 32 (2): 307–328.

Engelhardt, Tom. 2006. "Shark and Awe." *Salon*. Accessed on March 10, 2006. Available at http://www.salon.com/opinion/feature/2006/03/10/sharks/

Fever, Peter D. and Gelpi, Christopher. 2004. *Choosing Your Battles: American Civil-Military Relations and the Use of Force*. Princeton, NJ: Princeton University Press.

Gray, Chris Hables. 1997. *Postmodern War: The New Politics of Conflict*. New York: Guilford Press.

Holsti, Ole R. 1998–1999. "A Widening Gap between the U.S. Military and Civilian Society? Some Evidence, 1976–1996." *International Security* 23 (3) (Winter): 5–42.

Roland, Alex and Shiman, Philip. 2002. *Strategic Computing: DARPA and the Quest for Machine Intelligence*. Cambridge, MA: MIT Press.

Segal, David R. and Mady Wechsler Segal. 2004. "America's Military Population," *Population Bulletin* 59 (4) (December): 3–17.

Singer, P.W. 2003. *Corporate Warriors: the Rise of the Privatized Military Industry*. Ithaca: Cornell University Press.

Xu, Shaohua Xu, Talwar, Sanjiv K., Hawley, Emerson S. Li, Lei and Chapin John K. 2004. "A Multi-Channel Telemetry System for Brain Microstimulation in Freely Roaming Animals," *Journal of Neuroscience Methods* 133 (1–2) (February): 57–63.

For Further Discussion

1. Although some contemporaries felt sure that the author of *The Red Badge of Courage* must have known the Civil War firsthand, Stephen Crane was born too late to have taken part in the conflict. Do you believe that Crane captured the realism of the war or is there some facet of the book (or Crane's style) that belies the fact that he was not battle-tested? Use your reading of the novel and your understanding of his biography to support your claims.

2. Many critics have debated whether Henry Fleming is a heroic character by the end of *The Red Badge of Courage* or whether his brave actions are tainted by Stephen Crane's ironic style. Look at the essays by Amy Kaplan and Weihong Julia Zhu and make an argument that defines Fleming as a self-willed hero, a self-deluded hero, or some characterization that falls in between those extremes.

3. Much of Henry Fleming's transformation over the course of the novel is motivated by his relationship to his comrades and military command. Using the arguments made in the essays by Robert M. Myers and Daniel Shanahan, discuss how Fleming's character (especially his cowardice and subsequent bravery) is shaped by this relationship. Do you think, as Shanahan does, that Stephen Crane had a larger purpose in portraying the army in the manner he does? Explain.

4. Stephen Crane relies heavily on Henry Fleming's limited viewpoint to illustrate his character's varied emotional reactions to the unfamiliar nature of war. John Horgan argues that most people should feel unfamiliar with war because the world is becoming more peaceful. Yet he is dumbfounded by a persistent belief in society that human

beings are intrinsically driven to fight each other. Do you believe that war is an innate part of human nature, or is it something that, as Horgan believes, can be defeated by humanity's better nature? Explain your reasoning.

5. Do you think Henry Fleming's journey could be replicated on a modern battlefield? What aspects of his character and his environment seem strikingly contemporary, and what elements of the story could never occur on today's battlefields? Use any of the essays from Chapters 2 and 3 to help frame your answer.

6. Part of what entrances readers of *The Red Badge of Courage* is the unvarnished depiction of the brutal and ugly face of war. Jason Royce Lindsey contends that conflict is becoming more acceptable today because the brutality is being erased by advances in technology and medicine. Do you agree with Lindsey's assessment that America is more tolerant of sending troops off to combat because of these advances? Give real-world examples of America's complacency or its continuing resistance to the urge to fight.

For Further Reading

Stephen Crane, *The Black Riders and Other Lines*. Gloucester, UK: Dodo, 1895.

———, *Maggie: A Girl of the Streets, and Other New York Writings*. New York: Random House, 1893.

———, *The Portable Stephen Crane*. Ed. Joseph Katz. New York: Penguin, 1977.

———, *War Is Kind*. New York: Bookman, 1899.

———, *Wounds in the Rain*. Stockbridge, MA: HardPress, 1900.

Shelby Foote, *Shiloh: A Novel*. New York: Vintage, 1952.

Gustav Hasford, *The Short-Timers*. New York: Bantam, 1979.

Harold Keith, *Rifles for Watie*. New York: HarperTeen, 1957.

Michael Shaara, *The Killer Angels*. New York: Ballantine, 1974.

Bibliography

Books

Daniel Aaron
The Unwritten War: American Writers and the Civil War. New York: Knopf, 1973.

Andrew J. Bacevich
The New American Militarism: How Americans Are Seduced by War. New York: Oxford University Press, 2005.

Michael Barton and Larry M. Logue, eds.
The Civil War Soldier: A Historical Reader. New York: New York University Press, 2002.

Maurice Bassan
Stephen Crane: A Collection of Critical Essays. Upper Saddle River, NJ: Prentice-Hall, 1967.

Dora L. Costa and Matthew E. Kahn
Heroes and Cowards: The Social Face of War. Princeton, NJ: Princeton University Press, 2008.

Joseph Allan Frank and George A. Reaves
Seeing the Elephant: Raw Recruits at the Battle of Shiloh. Champaign: University of Illinois Press, 2003.

Eugene Jarecki
The American Way of War: Guided Missiles, Misguided Men, and a Republic in Peril. New York: Free Press, 2008.

David Kilcullen
The Accidental Guerrilla: Fighting Small Wars in the Midst of a Big One. New York: Oxford University Press, 2009.

Lee Clark
Mitchell, ed.
New Essays on "The Red Badge of Courage." New York: Cambridge University Press, 1986.

Michael
Robertson
Stephen Crane, Journalism, and the Making of Modern American Literature. New York: Columbia University Press, 1997.

P.W. Singer
Wired for War: The Robotics Revolution and Conflict in the 21st Century. New York: Penguin, 2009.

Eric Solomon
Stephen Crane: From Parody to Realism. Cambridge, MA: Harvard University Press, 1967.

Robert W.
Stallman
Stephen Crane: A Biography. New York: George Braziller, 1968.

Alvin and
Heidi Toffler
War and Anti-War. New York: Warner, 1995.

Periodicals

Harold Beaver
"Stephen Crane: The Hero as Victim," *Yearbook of English Studies,* 1982.

Christopher
Benfey
"Badges of Courage and Cowardice: A Source for Crane's Title," *Stephen Crane Studies,* 1997.

John S. Brown
"War, Peace and Army Transformation," *Army,* July 2009.

Peter W. Chiarelli and Stephen M. Smith	"Learning from Our Modern Wars: The Imperatives of Preparing for a Dangerous Future," *Military Review*, September/October 2007.
John Clendenning	"Visions of War and Versions of Manhood," special issue, *War, Literature, and the Arts: An International Journal of the Humanities*, 1999.
Guerric DeBona	"Masculinity on the Front: John Huston's *The Red Badge of Courage* (1951) Revisited," *Cinema Journal*, Winter 2003.
Chris Hedges	"War Is Sin," *Catholic New Times*, June 8, 2009.
Andrew Lawson	"The Red Badge of Class: Stephen Crane and the Industrial Army," *Literature and History*, November 2005.
Robert McIlvaine	"Henry Fleming Wrestles with an Angel," *Pennsylvania English*, 1985.
Jesse Thomas Moore Jr.	"Causes Won, Lost, and Forgotten: How Hollywood and Popular Art Shape What We Know About the Civil War," *Journal of American History*, June 2009.
Joshua Muravchik	"Winds of War," *Wall Street Journal*, June 25, 2007.
Gervase Phillips	"Was the American Civil War the First Modern War?" *History Review*, December 2006.

Stuart Reid   "What Is It Good For?" *American Conservative*, May 18, 2009.

Stephen   "Blood Brothers," *American Interest*,
Peter Rosen   July/August 2009.

Michael Schaefer   "Stephen Crane in the Time of Shock and Awe: Teaching *The Red Badge of Courage* During the Iraq War," *Stephen Crane Studies*, Fall 2004.

John Talbott   "Combat Trauma in the American Civil War," *History Today*, March 1996.

Stanley Wertheim   "*The Red Badge of Courage* and Personal Narratives of the Civil War," *American Literary Realism, 1870–1910*, vol. 6, 1973.

Howard Zinn   "A Just Cause and a Just War," *Progressive*, July 2009.

Index